A BALLANTIN

In early 1968, rioting students brought one of
Europe's most successful post-war governments
to its knees and galvanized sections of the
working class for a spontaneous revolution.
What was Paris like, day by day, in those weeks
of crisis? What is the truth about police
terror-tactics in the vicious street battles
that shook the capital? Why were the revolutionary
leaders—Sauvageot, Geismar, and Daniel Cohn-Bendit
—so hostile to the ideas and style of the Old Left?
Have the student militants a coherent message for
the future? Above all, is this revolution in
a supposedly stable nation a forecast of the
politics of the 1970's?

As correspondents for *The Observer*, Patrick
Seale and Maureen McConville observed from
the inside the tactics and strategies on both
sides of the barricades. From conversations
and vivid eye-witness reports they have
constructed a trenchant analysis of the roots
of the crisis, its hectic course, and its
implications for France and the western
world.

About the Authors

Patrick Seale and Maureen McConville are at present
Paris correspondents for the British journal, *The Observer*.

PATRICK SEALE was born in Northern Ireland and
spent his early years in the Middle East. Educated
in Britain, he read Philosophy and Psychology at
Balliol College, Oxford, then took an Economics
diploma at London University. He is a senior
scholar of St Anthony's College, Oxford. He
succeeded Kim Philby, the master spy, as the
Observer and *Economist* Middle East correspondent,
collaborated with Mrs Eleanor Philby in writing
her book *Kim Philby: the Spy I Married* (1968),
and is at present working on an exhaustive political
biography of Kim Philby. He is also the author of
a scholarly study on contemporary Middle East
political history, *The Struggle for Syria* (second
edition 1967).

MAUREEN McCONVILLE was born in England of Irish
extraction and educated at a convent school in
Lancashire and Bedford College, London, where
she read English. She has worked for a football
pool and a mental institution, but her chief activities
have been in journalism; first on the British
provincial press, then at O.E.C.D., Paris, and,
currently, on the *Observer*. She is a left-wing
Catholic absorbed by international politics, but
only if and when politics is about people.

RED FLAG/ BLACK FLAG

French Revolution 1968

photographs by Chris Marker and others

Patrick Seale and Maureen McConville

Ballantine Books
New York

To The Observer who enabled us
to witness the May Revolution

Contents

Foreword

The May Revolution of 1968 was a disturbance in French society on a scale to break the seismograph. It was the sort of event which sets your mind reeling for months afterwards as you try to make sense of it.

This book is an attempt to do three things: to relate what actually happened in those turbulent weeks; to set the explosion in its context of French politics; and finally to single out what we take to be the original and creative features of the situation. These are our 'Experiments in Revolution' in the centre of the book. They are glimpses of the new order which for a moment replaced the old: they are strictly speaking what the Revolution was about.

The French tremor was more than an aberrant lapse in the confident forward march of Western industrial society. The point is that it nearly overthrew the most majestic government in Europe. Its lessons must be carefully pondered because they carry a hint of what politics in the West may be like in the 1970s.

Paris, 1 August 1968

P.S.
M.M.

Note on Sources

One of the advantages of writing instant history is that the makers of it tend to be still around, and sometimes agree to talk. We have not been able to interview General de Gaulle, but many of his opponents were more accessible. We are especially grateful to Pierre Frank, Jean-François Godchau, Marc Kravetz, Alain Krivine, and Michael Recanati for keeping us informed of their activities throughout the crisis. We would also like to thank the many other observers of the French scene—politicians, diplomats, journalists, students—who were kind enough to share their views with us. We have not mentioned them by name to spare them the responsibility of being associated with our interpretation of events. But it is a risk we hope he will forgive us taking in the case of Robert Stephens, our colleague on *The Observer,* to whom we are particularly indebted.

In writing this little book, we have made unabashed use of the French national press, and of fringe youth-group publications, such as *Action, Avant-garde Jeunesse, Servir le Peuple*, and *Révoltes*. We have read mountains of tracts and pamphlets. But there is a debt which we should like to acknowledge above all others—that which we owe to that incomparable bourgeois newspaper, *Le Monde*. When the history of journalism in the twentieth century comes to be written, *Le Monde* will surely figure on a splendid and lonely peak. Others clearly found it as riveting as we did: its circulation soared from 429,099 on 22 March 1968 (the birthday of Daniel Cohn-Bendit's movement) to 688,300 on 30 May (the day General de Gaulle saved himself from the abyss). Where all are excellent, it may seem unjust to single out a few, but in looking for the meaning of the May crisis we found particularly penetrating the writings of:

Raymond Barrillon, Pierre Drouin, Maurice Duverger, Jacques Fauvet, André Fontaine, Frédéric Gaussen, Bertrand Girod de l'Ain, Guy Herzlich, Jean Lacouture, Michel Legris, Edgar Morin, Joanine Roy, Alain Touraine, Pierre Viansson-Ponté.

Short Glossary
of Revolutionary Jargon

amphi. Short for *amphithéâtre*, a university lecture hall; natural forum during the Revolution for the practice of direct democracy.

anar. Short for *anarchiste*; contributed black flags and joyful nonsense to the events of May.

autogestion. Self-management; a state of affairs, hard to define in practice, in which students or workers or what-have-you take sole charge of themselves.

chienlit. Two meanings, neither much in use: bed-messing; or, a carnival mask. Revived by General de Gaulle in his first dismissive comment on the Revolution: *'Oui à la réforme, non à la Chienlit!'*

chinois. A member of a pro-Chinese 'groupuscule' (see below); more generally, a Maoist.

cogestion. Management by a partnership of interested parties; in university terms, of students and teachers.

comité. The basic unit of revolutionary action; thousands sprang up.

contestation. A key word meaning to challenge, to cast doubt upon, to strip naked with criticism. *Contestation* is usually *permanente* or *globale*, meaning that no quarter is allowed the enemy.

démocratie directe. Opposed to bourgeois, parliamentary democracy. The base, source of all authority, exercises permanent control over its leaders and representatives, revoking them at will; anyone can at any time speak from the floor.

enragés. Used, in 1793, to describe an extreme revolutionary group led by Jacques Roux which had considerable influence on the *sansculottes*; applied, in 1968, to Daniel Cohen-Bendit and his troublesome friends at Nanterre, and triumphantly taken up by them.

forces de l'ordre. Euphemism for armed police.

groupuscule. A tiny group; term used pejoratively by the authorities to refer to the small political factions which detonated the Revolution. (The students riposte, marching in their tens of thousands, was to cry: *Nous sommes un groupuscule.*)

L'Huma. Short for *L'Humanité,* the daily organ of the French Communist Party.

libre circulation. In university hostels, the right to entertain a member of the opposite sex in one's bedroom.

manif. Short for *manifestation,* a demonstration.

mot d'ordre. Slogan, directive, order of the day issued by a leader to his followers.

militer. To be politically active; to go in for political agitation.

militant. An active member of a political formation.

occupation. A 'sit-in'.

pavé. A cobblestone, ammo for insurgents.

pègre. The underworld; alleged by the authorities to be responsible for the disturbances. (The students' riposte was: *Nous sommes tous la pègre.*)

prise de conscience. To enter a state of critical awareness about something or other.

réac. Short for *réactionnaire.*

société de consommation. Consumer society, mesmerized by material welfare.

structures. Another key word, meaning organizational framework, chain of command, power relationship.

Some Confusing Initials and Assorted Dramatis Personae

Political Youth Organizations

JCR. Jeunesse communiste révolutionnaire (Trotskyist; followers of Pierre Frank).

FER. Fédération des étudiants révolutionnaires (used to be CLER–Comité de liaison des étudiants révolutionnaires). (Trotskyist; followers of Pierre Lambert.)

UJC(M–L). Union des jeunesses communistes marxistes-léninistes (Pro-Chinese).

UEC. Union des étudiantes communistes (Orthodox Communists).

Occident. (Right-wing strong-arm boys.)

Political Movements and Fronts

22 March. Daniel Cohn-Bendit's Nanterre-based 'spontaneous' movement.

3 May. A short-lived, Paris-based, front of high-minded Marxists, mainly university research workers. (Grew out of the MAU–Mouvement d'action universitaire.)

CVN. Comité Vietnam national. An anti-Vietnam War protest 'front', which helped spread and mobilize left-wing anti-American sentiment.

Some Student and Teachers' Unions

UNEF. Union national des étudiants de France. (Left-wing controlled; acted as spokesman and coordinator of student protest.)

FNEF. Fédération nationale des étudiants de France. (Right-wing rival organization.)

SNESup. Syndicat national de l'enseignement supérieur. (Left-wing-led university teachers' union, active in Revolution.)

FEN. Fédération de l'éducation nationale. (Principal federation of teachers' unions.)

Secondary School Political Organizations

CAL. Comité d'action lycéen. (Extreme left school boy and girl factions which mobilized teenagers during Revolution; grew out of the CLVs – Comités lycées Vietnam.)

MJC. Mouvement de la jeunesse communiste. (Orthodox Communist school groups.)

Trade Unions

CGT. Confédération générale du travail. (Communist-led; most powerful trade union federation.)

CFDT. Confédération française et démocratique du travail. (Second most powerful; formerly linked to Catholic Church.)

FO. Force Ouvrière (third most powerful; split off from CGT when latter fell under Communist control.)

CFC. Confédération française des cadres (white-collar and junior executive federation.)

Political Parties

UDR. Union pour la défense de la Republique (appellation under which Gaullists fought June '68 elections).

UDVe. Union démocratique pour la Cinquième République (the Gaullist party before the elections).

Independent Republicans. (Valéry Giscard d'Estaing's parliamentary group.)

PCF. Parti communiste français (referred to in the text as the CPF).

FGDS. (M. François Mitterrand's socialist alliance, composed of three political 'families':
    – Guy Mollet's SFIO (Section française de l'internationale ouvrière);
    – the Radicals;
    – the Convention des institutions républicaines (a gathering of political clubs).

PDM. Progrès et démocratie moderne (a left-centre group, led by M. Jacques Duhamel).

PSU. Parti socialiste unifié (a splinter group on the extreme left of the social democratic spectrum).

Extremist Political Parties

PCI. Parti communiste internationaliste (French branch of the Fourth International – Trotskyist).

OCI. Organisation communiste internationaliste (rival Trotskyist faction, not affiliated to the Fourth International).

PCMLF. Parti communiste marxiste-léniniste de France (pro-Chinese).

Peasant Organizations

FNSEA. Fédération nationale des syndicats d'exploitants agricoles.

CNJA. Centre national des jeunes agriculteurs.

1   Revolting Students

Two hours before dawn on Monday, March 18, 1968, a left-wing student commando crossed the Seine to the fashionable Right Bank and, with small explosive charges, blew in the plate-glass windows of the Paris offices of the Chase Manhattan Bank, the Bank of America, and Trans World Airlines. A couple of nights later it was the turn of the American Express. By Friday morning the police, acting swiftly to quell these anti-Vietnam War gestures, had rounded up two young men and three schoolboys, all members of extremist organizations.

That same evening, March 22, 1968, a meeting was called at the University of Paris annex of Nanterre to protest against the arrests. Late that night, after the speeches, a body of demonstrators swarmed up the staircase of the tower block on the campus, to the administrative offices on the eighth floor, bursting open locked doors on their way up. They sat down and formed themselves spontaneously into a sort of students' council, debating with growing excitement and sense of purpose until the early hours of the morning. For months the authorities had denied these young militants the right to bring politics onto the campus. Now they felt they had grabbed what they wanted. A motion approving their action was put to the vote: 142 were for it, 2 against, and 3 abstained. The meeting broke up with the birth of a new force. To begin with, it called itself the 142, but it was to gain international notoriety as the Movement of March 22. The detonator had worked. The student revolt was off the ground.

This incident, unfolding almost unnoticed in a single week in spring, illustrates the key features of the revolution it triggered off: the boldness and strategic sense of the student leaders; the speed with which they reacted to events; their philosophy of direct action and persistent provocation; their courting of police repression as a lever to raise support among the mass of uncommitted. It also illustrates the fusing, with devastating effect, of two great currents at work in French youth: a political current focused on the Vietnam War, that great mobilizer of left-wing militancy, and another current, which had swelled up within the French educational system, feeding powerfully on its inadequacies. There was not much that was haphazard about the attacks on American property in Paris and their immediate repercussions in Nanterre.

From the very beginning of the revolution, one question above all others interested the public: Was the conflagration which spread like a bush fire across France spontaneous, or was it engineered by a band of conspirators? The answer is that it was both. The revolution would not have occurred without a hard core of revolutionaries of extremely high quality; they were good at both thinking and acting. They were the yeast in the dough of the student body. But when the loaf was baked, there was no separating the dough from the yeast. It had done its work.

A tiny revolutionary avant-garde detonated a large-scale spontaneous movement of student protest. This mass, generating its own dynamic, could be only loosely manipulated and controlled by the revolutionary core. It clashed with the police, threw up barricades, bred a legend of heroism, occupied the universities. The students' fighting example then fired the workers to strike and occupy in turn. This was the next and vital stage, longed for by the revolutionaries but only indirectly brought about by them. It was as if the French industrial working class, lulled by the prizes of a consumer society, had suddenly relearned from the students forgotten traditions of militancy. When the Great Strike paralyzed France and President de Gaulle was silent, the politicians jumped in to give a final blow to a regime they thought was doomed.

At every stage of this process, from the moment of detonation to the collapse of the revolution, the avant-garde was at full stretch, dashing from front to front with demonic energy, setting off new explosive charges, issuing fresh battle orders, trying to direct the vast army it had set in motion. But by its own admission, the army was too big for it. In sum, there was a conspiracy, but it was soon drowned in an impulsive tidal wave of liberty, equality, fraternity. This is an analysis given by the conspirators themselves. They make no secret of their revolutionary strategy. At the height of the May crisis, their chief spokesman, the student leader Daniel Cohn-Bendit, gave the game away with extraordinary candor. He was interviewed by Jean-Paul Sartre for the Paris left-wing weekly *Le Nouvel Observateur* (May 20, 1968). Sartre, like a cub reporter, put the questions, Cohn-Bendit, in a dazzling performance for a twenty-three-year-old, gave a lecture on how to make a revolution.

There was no question, he said, of overthrowing bourgeois society at one fell swoop. The tactic was to stage a number of revolutionary shocks, each setting off an irreversible process of change. These actions were the work of an activist minority, strongly grounded in revolutionary theory. Their role was to act as a detonator without attempting to control the process they unleashed. The strength of their movement was precisely that it rested on an element of uncontrollable spontaneity. Students had to give an example to workers, but the marriage of students and workers could only take place in joint combat. The immediate objective was not to reform capitalist society, but to attempt a public break with it. Such a revolt could not last, but it provided a fleeting glimpse of what was possible, of what could be.

Why was Nanterre, in the winter of 1967–68, the principal center of student agitation in France? It was not just that among its 15,000 students was a dynamic teddy bear called Cohn-Bendit. Nanterre itself, intended by the Ministry of Education as a blueprint for the universities of the future, became a blueprint for revolution. An austere composition of glass and steel cubes, it was built at speed in the early sixties to take pressure off the teeming ant heap of the *Quartier Latin*. Its first buildings were opened in 1964, when 2,300 students were admitted. By 1968 this figure had mushroomed sixfold, an ominous index to the rocketing French student population.

The heart of the problem is the French open-door policy to university entrance: Anyone who scrapes through the fearsome baccalaureate—summit of the secondary school system—can go on to a university. No further exam is required to get a place. This extreme liberality, coupled with the postwar demographic boom, caused a staggering inflation in student numbers: in 1946, 123,000; in 1961, 202,000; in 1968, 514,000. These hordes, marching inexorably into cramped lecture rooms, were the nightmare of the planners. "The dam will break one day if we do nothing," warned Christian Fouchet, Minister of Education, addressing a national congress on education at Caen in November, 1966.*

Panic-stricken, the planners thought only of bricks and mortar, neglecting the less tangible amenities that make a university education worthwhile. The sheer pressure of numbers blotted out everything else. It was like inviting a football crowd to a tea party—the hostess never met the

* *L'Université Face à sa réforme*, pp. 176–77. A report on the congress.

guests; the crockery was broken; the front garden trampled into mud. Under the weight, the universities, particularly the swollen Sorbonne, changed their character from small elitist clubs to inefficient, squalid factories of education, where everything was sacrificed to the simple problem of getting everyone in. Student-teacher relationships collapsed; university administrators were swamped, libraries and laboratories overrun; to be sure of a place on a crowded bench for a lecture of their choice, students at the Sorbonne would sometimes sit through the previous hour's instruction in a different field.

France is now thinking of introducing a selection system for university entrance. For one thing, the open-door policy has proved intellectually disastrous: Between a half and a third of the students fail to get a degree. In Britain, where entrance is stiff and competitive, 95 percent are graduated. The French system is wasteful because a savage weeding out does in fact operate at the end of the first year, when some 50 percent of the students drop out. What this means is that far too great a proportion of resources—teachers, buildings, funds—is deployed in coping with a flood of low-grade freshmen, many of whom never make it. Alain Peyrefitte, the young Minister of Education who lost his job during the student revolt, saw the problem coming but could not act in time. In 1967 he said, "It is as if we organized a shipwreck in order to pick out the best swimmers."

In spite of a sixfold increase in state spending on education in fifteen years, the French record can be summed up as too little and too late. It was not really until 1960 that the scale of the problem was grasped, only then that a massive recruitment of teachers was ordered. Four new universities—at Rouen, Amiens, Rheims, and Orléans— were created as a counterattraction to the capital, and in Paris itself two wholesale markets—one for hides and skins, the other for wine—became the sites of new extensions to the creaking Sorbonne. The Halle aux Cuirs in the Rue de

Censier became the overspill faculty of letters. (Censier during the May Revolution was as firm a bastion of insurgency as the Sorbonne itself; it was the first university building in France actually seized and occupied by the students.) The new science faculty at the Halle aux Vins on the Quai St.-Bernard—an experiment in raw concrete brutalism—was incomplete by 1968 but was already housing more students than it was meant to hold when finished.

Outside the center of Paris, in the postwar-built suburban belt, the planners put two residential campuses: one at Orsay, the other at Nanterre. The big decentralized residential campus on the American model, isolated from the distractions of the Latin Quarter, was the remedy for overcrowding on which the ministry pinned its hopes. The plan was that in ten years, half the students would live in. On the drawing boards, a necklace of new university sites was thrown around Paris to relieve its congestion: Montesson to the west; Pontoise to the northwest; Versailles and Trappes to the southwest; Tigery and Lieusaint to the southeast; Noisy-le-Grand to the east. These were to be the campuses of the 1980's. But the government has been slow at pushing through the necessary land purchases, and still more discouraging, no clear decision has yet been made on what type of educational institution is planned. Are they to be old-style faculties? More fashionable interdisciplinary establishments? Institutes of technology? A choice must clearly be made before the architects can get to work.

But the student revolt of May, 1968, has thrown doubt on the whole idea of the campus—at least in its present French form. French students do not want to live isolated from the society about them, now undergoing such profound changes under the impact of industrialization. They want to live in a community, not a barracks. At Nanterre, for example, the campus was dumped into a social vacuum by a planner's blueprint. Virtually nothing was done to give coherence to a population more than 15,000 strong. There

could be no greater contrast between the intensely attrac-
tive teeming café life of the Latin Quarter—everyone's
dream of liberated and articulate youth—and the bleak,
hygienic functionalism of Nanterre. Speaking from bitter
knowledge, the Nanterre sociologist Alain Touraine noted
that the big new twentieth-century student campus isolates
students in the way workers are isolated in American company towns. The student crowd is born, as dense and faceless as an industrial proletariat, with its own grievances, its
own leaders, its growing sense of its own power.

Nanterre is a graveyard of lost illusions. It was to be a
bold experiment, a break with the French past. Big names
left the Sorbonne to teach there; money was poured into it.
But it has since been the cause of much gnashing of ministerial teeth. It consists of a faculty of letters (which includes
the explosive department of sociology), a faculty of law
and economics, a restaurant, and segregated residential
blocks for boys and girls, facing each other squarely across
a no-man's-land: "Architectural incompetence . . . or
sadism?" asked one reporter. A magnificent Olympic-size
swimming pool has recently been added, but there are no
common rooms, no cultural facilities, and the library block
is still unfinished.

Above all, the context in which all this is springing up
is deeply disturbing. There is no sense of enclosure. The
ugliest features of the outside world are allowed to intrude.
On one side the campus is literally overhung by a vast cliff
of low-cost housing, a wall of mean living blotting out the
horizon. These shabby municipal flats are largely inhabited
by immigrant labor, Spanish or Algerian, at the squalid bottom end of the wage scale. The morals of the student community could not escape infection from the misery of their
neighbors—particularly for the 1,200 who lived on the
campus, divided almost equally between boys and girls.
When the student hostels first opened, parents were reluctant to send their daughters because of the nearby shanty-

towns. Soon a reputation for scandalous goings-on grew up about Nanterre; there were hints of free love, drug taking, prostitution. *Les demoiselles de Nanterre* were featured in the scurrilous press. These irregularities (there was some truth under the exaggerations) were connected with the problem which plagues all French universities: the "phantom students" who register not so much to study as for the ambiguous social status conferred by being a student, for the cheap rooms and meals, for the passport of the *carte d'étudiant*. This abuse flourishes in the laxity of a system under strain.

Beyond the cheap housing which rings Nanterre is an industrial wasteland, shabby and scarred. There are railway sidings, the gaping trench of a planned express metro, the gash of a new highway under construction. Underfoot there is mud and gravel and patches of sparse grass. There are few trees. Studies are pursued to the grinding of earth-moving machines and the shunting of freight trains.

If these charmless surroundings helped create a revolutionary situation, another factor was the paradox that Nanterre is probably the most bourgeois university in France (in a university population still overwhelmingly middle class, less than 10 percent of the students come from working-class families as against at least 30 percent in Britain). Nanterre is no deprived, underprivileged community. The catchment zone includes the chic sixteenth and seventeenth *arrondissements* of Paris, the plush middle-class dormitories of Neuilly and the Bois de Boulogne. These were for the most part the children of the well-off, more modish, trendy, expensive, than the Sorbonne inhabitants. It is the girls who give the show away—culottes, glossy leather, mini-skirts, boots—driving up in Mini Coopers to the vast parking lots on the campus. Rebellious sentiment is more obvious among the boys: long hair; square spectacles; Che Guevara beards. The picture in Nanterre in May was lots and lots of painted dollies cohabiting with unkempt revolutionaries.

For most of the students at Nanterre, education was not a necessary stepladder to social promotion; their status was already secure. It was the planting of revolutionary ideas in a context of arrogant social confidence which was perhaps most responsible for creating the peculiar Nanterre climate of daredevilry, contempt for authority, and a sort of idle openness to reckless suggestions.

Irresponsibility is built into the French educational system (at least as it existed before the great May shake-up). Virtually no powers of decision are in local hands; all administrative decisions, all budgetary allocations, all staff appointments are the exclusive prerogative of a distant and faceless bureaucracy in Paris. A French university is like a factory in Russia: It works to norms ordained by the center. All twenty-three universities in the country are state-run, on rigidly standardized lines, like a government department. The local administrative staff is impotent, the students resentful, their mutual relations hostile. Discussion is pointless since decisions are taken elsewhere. Both students and teachers are powerless. As a result, grievances —instead of being eroded by negotiation and practical reform—are repressed, then acted out in explosions of collective hysteria. This is one explanation for the combustible material which Cohn-Bendit and his friends found lying to hand at Nanterre.

What are these student grievances? Of course, there are a host of petty ones to do, for instance, with overcrowding and poor amenities and transportation problems. But there are others which run deeper. In the crisis conditions of gross overcrowding and in the failure of an old-fashioned university system to adapt to the needs of a rapidly changing and increasingly technological society, neither teachers nor students really know what they are at the university for. To more and more students this year, Nanterre seemed neither a preparation for a career nor a coherent cultural community. There was deep frustration among the students at their powerlessness to share in making decisions affecting their lives. The state ran the universities with as little imagination as it ran the postal service. What the students wanted above all was to force the state to consult them at their level. This was not always a conscious wish, but it was a profound motive for revolt.

An allied discontent was the fact that the authorities treated the students like children. The rector in many universities is a sort of stern foster parent, appointed by Paris; many teachers, on their professional pedestals, expect deference, refuse dialogue; the rules and regulations governing student life bear little relation to present-day attitudes and precocious maturity. Some bear little relation to common sense. Under the strict rules, students are not allowed to pin up photographs in their rooms or move furniture. On no account must their personalities be imprinted on their surroundings. No politics or propaganda is, in principle, allowed. The explanation for these curiously insensitive provisions is that the regulations were taken over from those framed for the *internat* (boarding department) of *lycées,* when the issue of the religious and political neutrality of state education aroused fierce passions.

As a fighting issue, symbolizing all their grievances, the students chose the question of strict segregation between boys' and girls' residential blocks. The young people wanted free access to one another's bedrooms, expressly forbidden by Paris decree and enforced on the spot by hostel wardens. Over the past three years the bedroom issue became as much a part of the students' charter as wage claims for an industrial union. The first revolt against segregation broke out at Antony, the biggest and oldest student residential complex in France, twenty minutes by train from the center of Paris. In the "red autumn" of 1965, 1,700 students forcibly prevented workmen from putting up a warden's

lodge in front of the girls' hostel. The rector called in the
police, who camped on the site till the building was completed. But for three months there were scuffles, demonstrations, overheated tempers. To calm the students, Paris
sacrificed the director at Antony, and in January, 1966, the
new man, Jacques Balland, introduced a more flexible but
unofficial ruling: Students over twenty-one could entertain
members of the opposite sex in their rooms; minors needed
written permission from their parents to enjoy the same
privilege (interestingly enough, 90 percent of the minors
got the permission). "The student problem is like decolo-
nization," the new liberal director declared. "We must de-
paternalize." Paris never made the new ruling official.

The bedroom revolt gained Nanterre in the spring of
1967, when, on the eve of the Easter holidays, parents
were horrified to learn that boys had invaded the corridors
of the girls' dormitories. There was talk of "free copula-
tion." To get out the boys—who showed every sign of staying—the authorities had to call in the fire brigade and the
police. Another director was sacked on orders from Paris.

On February 14, 1968—St. Valentine's Day—a rebellion in favor of "free circulation" between boys' and girls'
hostels spread like wildfire throughout France. In nearly
every students' residence the boys stormed the girls' block
to protest against segregation. The success of the protest
was due to preplanning by UNEF, the students' union. It
was the first time UNEF had intervened on a national
scale in the students' hostels. (The movement reached the
American Pavilion at the Paris Cité Universitaire on April
2—one of the last fortresses to fall.) Everywhere the deans,
waiting for directives from Paris, did nothing, except in
Nantes, Nice, and Montpellier, where the police were called
in—only to provide the students with a further cause for
militancy. In Montpellier, girls joined forces with boys in
throwing the police out, while in Nantes the rebels sacked
the rector's office, before being overpowered. A week later

the harassed Minister of Education, Alain Peyrefitte, came up with a new ruling: Girls would be allowed, until 11 P.M., into the rooms of boys over twenty-one. But it was to be one-way traffic—boys would not be allowed into girls' rooms. The minister explained: "Boys and girls don't run the same risks. Girls must have a free choice. To admit boys into girls' blocks is to expose *all* the girls to danger." "Hypocrisy!" cried the students. Peyrefitte's concessions seemed wildly daring to some university administrators; to the students they were totally inadequate. The ministry had not grasped that access to one another's bedrooms was only a symbol of the students' desire to be treated as adults. They wanted the freedoms enjoyed by the rest of the nation, political freedoms such as those of association, information, and expression, as well as sexual freedoms.

Such were some of the roots of the student exasperation which grew into something entirely new—a political challenge, not only to the bourgeois university, but to the bourgeois state.

All students are Bolshie; students of sociology are Bolshier than most. If this phenomenon is true anywhere, it is true at Nanterre, where the sociology department was the nursery of the revolution. It is a discipline which, by its very nature, makes those who study it critical of and questioning about the society in which they live. In addition, hanging over the department was the grim cloud of graduate unemployment: In France there are extremely few established outlets for sociologists. It was in the sociology department that were first militantly formulated the student objections to the way teaching at Nanterre was done, to the content of the curricula, to the old plague of overcrowding. In agreement with their teachers—humaner than the general run—the Nanterre sociologists staged a strike on November 17, 1967.

The strikers did not go on holiday. They came to the

lecture halls, not to listen to an academic lecture, but determined to thrash out with their teachers and the university authorities a program of reforms. The movement spread to the whole faculty, involving 10,000 students, and lasted ten days. It ended with what seemed a substantial achievement: the setting up of a joint teachers-students committee to draft reforms and submit them to the ministry in Paris. But there were colossal obstacles. What the strikers really wanted, although they did not put it this way, was local autonomy, perhaps an essential precondition for a successful university. They wanted to devise their own methods of work and research, to revamp the curricula in the light of new knowledge, to specialize as they pleased. These ambitions clashed with the obscurantist views of some of the professors and, more fundamentally, with the basic objection that decisions of such magnitude could only be taken in Paris. "This is a committee," one of the professors said, "in which *everything* can be discussed, because nothing can be decided."

Gradually it became evident that the joint committee was getting nowhere. A split developed between a reformist majority, preoccupied by practical worries about jobs and books and laboratories, and a militant minority which undercut the whole notion of piecemeal reform and denounced the concept of the university as servant of the technocratic state. Disillusion with the committee strengthened the militants' hand. It was at this point that the strong current of criticism which sprang from the study of sociology merged with and was reinforced by a current of Marxism, providing the rebels with an ideological critique of the bourgeois state. The reformists, eager to tinker with an archaic university machine, crumbled away before the glamor of those who said that bourgeois life was mean and oppressive, that bourgeois careers were derisory, that it was not integration into this corrupt society that students should seek, but a total contestation of it. By January, 1968, any pretense of constructive contacts between teachers and students had to he abandoned. Sober talk of reform was lost in a climate of rising hysteria. The dean, Pierre Grappin, quite a distinguished scholar, became the target for gross personal attacks.

And so the *enragés,* the wild ones, emerged, total critics of their community, totally insolent, totally without remorse. Because they were weak in numbers, their basic strategy was provocation. They were a horrible enemy for anyone in authority. They christened themselves *enragés* as a tribute to Jacques Roux, "the priest of the sans-culottes"—the original *enragé* who rallied to the Revolution of 1789, became a member of the Paris Commune, but was condemned to death by a revolutionary tribunal in 1794. He stabbed himself on hearing the sentence.

Soon the *enragés* became so troublesome, so disruptive of peace and quiet, that it was felt that surely the authorities must act against them. Rumors spread that police informers in plain clothes had infiltrated the campus to take sly photographs of troublemakers. The authorities were said to be compiling a blacklist. The National Union of French Students (UNEF), springing to the defense of its members, issued a protest. "Rot!" said the dean, "No such blacklist exists." But the idea had been planted in suspicious young minds.

The climate was therefore pretty electric when, later in January, the Minister of Youth and Sports, François Missoffe, came down to Nanterre to inaugurate his ministry's pet project: the splendid new swimming pool, part of a million-dollar sports complex. He was walking into a hornets' nest. There were rumblings of outrage in his cortege when it was discovered that the *enragés* had issued tracts announcing "Vandal Orgies" at the swimming pool for the time the minister was due to cut the ribbon. The minister himself was somewhat unnerved to see obscene inscriptions, including an enormous phallus, scrawled on the walls on his official route. As it happened, the ceremony was uneventful; there was no bacchanal of nymphs and satyrs. But as the minister was on the point of leaving, a bouncy, slouching young redhead stepped from the crowd and addressed M. Missoffe in the confident, hectoring tone so soon to become familiar. Cohn-Bendit has the sort of chest which makes a microphone superfluous.

"Mr. Minister, you've drawn up a report on French youth six hundred pages long [a reference to a ministry document which had just appeared]. But there isn't a word in it about our sexual problems. Why not?"

"I'm quite willing to discuss the matter with responsible people, but you're clearly not one of them. I myself prefer sport to sexual education. If you have sexual problems, I suggest you jump in the pool." The minister had lost his temper.

"That's what the Hitler Youth used to say," Cohn-Bendit retorted brazenly.

The exchange made him a hero, but fearing reprisals, he wrote to the minister explaining that his interjection was not to be construed in any personal sense. Missoffe's daughter was, as it turned out, a student at Nanterre and served to effect a reconciliation between Cohn-Bendit and her father. The youth was invited to take tea with the minister and made his apology.

As is now well known, Cohn-Bendit was born in France of German refugee parents. He returned to school in Germany in his early teens and at eighteen opted for German nationality. He was in France on a renewable visa. His troublemaking at Nanterre brought him to the attention of the Ministry of the Interior, and he was due to appear in February before a special police committee concerned with deciding on expulsion orders. But Missoffe wished to make no complaint, and the Ministry of the Interior, on reflection, came to the view that any disciplinary action against

Cohn-Bendit was a matter for the university, not for the state.

But these high-level decisions were not generally known, and rumors spread on the campus that Cohn-Bendit was going to be expelled because of the Missoffe incident. There was a curious ambiguity in the militants' attitude: They feared repression and yet courted it. They wanted to provoke the authorities, but not to the extent of being totally crushed. In their minds, the Cohn-Bendit affair became fused with the suspicion that police informers were active inside the university. The *enragés'* counterattack was in characteristic style—original, cheeky, effective. Cameras were turned on the police, the photographs blown up, pinned on placards, and jeeringly paraded up and down in the hall of the Sociology Building on the morning of January 26. There were hasty confabulations in the administration block. Political demonstrations were not allowed on the campus, but how was this ruling to be enforced, when the crowd of rebels, now some fifty strong, seemed to be growing larger and noisier every minute? An administrative officer hurried down to call the students to order. There was a scuffle. He and his assistants were pushed about. Dean Grappin was informed, reached for his telephone, and called for police help.

It was about eleven o'clock before half a dozen *gardiens de la paix* arrived on the scene. One look at the mob, and they decided this was too big for them to handle: They must call for reinforcements. An hour later four vanloads of armed police drove up, and Grappin signed the paper authorizing them to enter the university precincts. Little did he know he was playing the *enragés'* game. Like guerrillas leading an infantry column into an ambush, the *enragés* pelted the police with anything that came to hand and, running before them, drew them onto the campus. At that precise moment the doors of the lecture halls were thrown open to release a thousand students for their mid-day break. Be-

fore their astonished eyes their fears of repression took concrete form: The police, the hated *flics,* were no longer a
rumor; they were a fact. Anger exploded like a fire bomb.
"Death to the dean!" they shouted. *"À bas les flics! Non à
l'université des flics! Nazis!"* Armed with benches as bat-
tering rams, chair legs, stones, and bottles, the student mob
drove into the police ranks, separating them, swamping
them, chasing them here and there across the gravel and
the thin grass by the swimming pool into the parking lots.
Windows were shattered, cars bashed about, men wounded
in both camps. Defeated, the police fled from the campus.
The *enragés* had become a rabble army.

The technique had worked in embryo; the strategy of direct action, detonated by a militant minority, had been put
to the test. Provocation had drawn repression, which, in
turn, had rallied mass support. But this time there was no
real takeoff, no organizational follow-up; no movement was
created, only a state of mind. Throughout February and
into March, Nanterre simmered, breaking out here and
there in a rash of incidents. It joined the rest of the country
for the girls' dormitory riot of February 14. The terminal
exams in social studies had to be canceled because of indiscipline. A group of *enragés* burst into a Spanish studies
seminar, brushed aside the teacher, and demanded signa-
tures for an anti-Franco resolution. A performance of Paul
Claudel's play *L'Otage* was broken up to cries of "Filthy
priest!" These were more or less unnoticed oscillations on
the seismograph, until the explosive bangs outside American buildings in Paris in the early hours of March 18 sent
the graph plunging wildly again.

We sketched at the opening of this chapter how the arrests which followed these explosions led to protest meetings at Nanterre and to the birth of Cohn-Bendit's March
22 Movement. Who were the arrested men? Two were in
their early twenties, three in their teens. The men were Nic-
olas Boulte, a leader of the *Comité Vietnam National*

(CVN), and Xavier Langlade, a student at Nanterre and a member of the *Jeunesse Communiste Révolutionnaire* (JCR). All three boys belonged to left-wing *Comités d' Action Lycéens* (CAL's)—school action committees. These initials—and many others—will become familiar to readers who stay with us. From the start the *enragés'* action was more political than anything else. So far we have tried to point to the grievances within the universities on which their movement fed. Their political ideas and fighting issues, their Marxism, the way their movement was powered by Vietnam protest—the whole tangle of left-wing student politics in France—must wait until the next chapter.

2   Latin Quarter Politics

LEFT-WING student politics in France are such a dense and dangerous jungle that only those raised in it ever really know their way about. In the undergrowth lurk bands of savage boys, armed with revolutionary dogmas—and sometimes sticks and stones. It is a climate far crueler than adult politics, demanding for survival great gifts and skills. Student leaders have to be able to think on their feet, to talk like angels, to know how to conduct a seminar and handle a mob. They must be expert theoreticians, as well as military tacticians. Because their forum is the street, they are more like gang leaders than parliamentarians. And all this at *fifteen!* The extraordinary feature of the May Revolution in Paris was the extreme youth of the rebel troops. If most members of the general staff were over twenty, much of the infantry came from school. Revolutionary ideas took hold of thousands of teen-agers in a way unmatched in any other European country. But French parents were slow to catch on. They saw nothing coming They imagined their children, bent over their homework, were still under the crippling spell of the baccalaureate. In a Normandy town a fifteen-year-old schoolgirl had been a revolutionary Communist for six months without arousing the slightest parental anxiety. "I thought it was a club!" her mother cried in horror, learning the truth in May. When the revolution came, it was as if every respectable middle-class family had a fifth columnist in its bosom. It was even rumored that Cabinet decisions were leaked to the rebels by the offspring of ministers.

Politics has conquered the young in France, absorbing energies which in other countries go into model aircraft building, ham radio, the pursuit of pop idols, sports. But it is politics of a special kind. Just as the parents knew nothing about it, so the established political parties—the great adult talking shops of left and right—failed to understand this ferment. A central point about the left-wing flood, which, overspilling French schools and universities in May, 1968, threatened to bring down the state itself, is that it grew up outside and against *all* the existing political parties—the Communist Party included. In sum, what this volcanic occurrence meant was that the parties had lost control of youth. Of course, most French political parties, like those in other countries, boast of some sort of youth policy and run groups for young people. This policy failed. These groups were mere skeletons. The boys and girls with ideas and energy and blood in their veins were militating elsewhere. They were on the hitherto neglected extreme left of the spectrum—well to the left of the Communist Party—in tiny, fierce, sectarian groupings of their own creation, identifiable by a jingle of initials meaningless to all but the initiates. This is not a uniquely French phenomenon; it is common to much of Europe and North America.

How many adults in the Western world, even those who reckon to be politically well informed, could write down on the back of a postcard the essential facts about the following?

Jeunesse Communiste Révolutionnaire (JCR)— France
Fédération des Étudiants Révolutionnaires (FER)— France

Union des Jeunesse Communistes (Marxistes-Léninistes) (UJC[M-L])—France

Radical Students Alliance (RSA)—Britain

Young Socialist Alliance (YSA)—United States

Young Socialist Forum (YSF)—Canada

Ligue des Jeunesses Socialistes du Quebec (LJSQ)—Canada

Sozialistischer Deutscher Studentenbund (SDS)—West Germany

Falcemartello (FM)—Italy

Jeune Garde Socialiste (JGS)—Belgium

Politeia—Holland

This is by no means a full list. One thing is certain—all these organizations have more in common with one another than with any other political setup. They are sister sects. They have sprung up, not as a result of an international conspiracy, but because many young people in the West have spontaneously come to the view that their parents' world is due for some pretty violent political surgery.

This radical current has arisen among intellectuals, not workers; in schools and universities, not factories. For one thing, there are more students than there used to be; countries like France, riding a demographic boom, are getting younger and younger, and more and more children are staying in school. For another, the new revolutionary spirit is supported by some moderately sophisticated analysis on theoretical lines of the present state of the world. Needless to say, the analysis does not always lead to the same conclusions. Ideological conflicts are sharp. Sometimes the protest is primitive and confused, as in the case of the Dutch *provos,* but usually there is a world view, expressed in suitably erudite and obscure Marxist jargon. Such speculations are not necessarily beyond the ken of factory workers, but they spring more naturally from minds sharpened in the Sorbonne. It should be said at once, however,

that the engrossing preoccupation of these insurgent intellectuals is, in fact, the working class. They yearn to link
up with it, to fertilize it, to restore it to what they consider
its original revolutionary vocation. So far such student-
worker links are few, in France as elsewhere; were they
to become widespread and strong, the old bourgeois world
would have to look smartly to its defenses.

For more than eighteen months during 1967 and 1968,
the left-wing student movements in the West spoke a common language: that of anti-American protest against the
Vietnam War. This is the common revolutionary coinage.
It is no exaggeration to say that without the war, these
groups would be greatly enfeebled, if they existed at all.
Vietnam has served them as a great recruiting slogan, but
it is something more. It is a key to their view of the world
situation: a decisive trial of strength between American
imperialism on the one hand and what they call the colonial revolution and the world workers' movement on the
other. Vietnam is the class struggle writ large; it is an in-
tegral part of the worldwide Socialist revolution they work
for.

Under the banner of "unconditional support for the
struggle of the Vietnam people," a dozen extremist youth
groups met in Brussels in March, 1967, to plan a joint
strategy and pool resources. They established a European
secretariat and governing body. In such ways are revolutionary ideas spread and contacts made that give coherence
to such scattered upheavals as the Berlin students' revolt,
the Grosvenor Square riot in London in March, 1968, the
Paris May Revolution. The *Comité Vietnam National*
(CVN) in France and the Vietnam Solidarity Campaign
(VSC) in Britain—both great mobilizers of young radical
opinion—are sisters beneath the skin.

In France the soaking of youth in politics took place in
the decade since the debunking of Stalin and the breakup
of the Stalinist monolith. The Soviet Union—clumsy, il-

liberal, persecuting intellectuals, still run on lines of political gangsterism; at the same time absorbed in its own economic interests, sacrificing world revolution to "peaceful coexistence" with the capitalist West—was no longer a pole of attraction for young radicals. In France this disillusion was expressed in angry rumblings by intellectuals inside the Communist Party, which remained unswervingly loyal to Moscow. The CPF's attitude to the Hungarian and Polish revolutions of 1956 led, for instance, to violent arguments in the party's student cells. To isolate these undisciplined intellectuals from the rest of the party, the CPF scrapped its existing youth organization, the UJRF (*Union de la Jeunesse Républicaine de France*), and replaced it by four new bodies, which split the young people into watertight compartments: boys, girls, peasants, and students. The new student group was named the *Union des Étudiants Communistes* (UEC)* of which we shall hear a good deal more.

Russia no longer attracted the young, but there were new idols. The Third World was now the center of attention, not the Soviet workers' state, the holy grail of Western Communists in the 1930's. The colonial revolution—the successive waves of revolutionary struggle which have shaken the postwar world in China, Korea, Algeria, Cuba, Vietnam —threw up heroes and ideas that deeply moved the imagination of the young, leading them to radical politics in a way nothing in their own society could. Thrilled by the guerrillas' example, young militants came to believe that imperialism could be attacked on its home ground, by its own working class—if only the working class could be provided with a revolutionary leadership. The advanced capitalist countries, dozing in affluence like a baby after its bottle, at last seemed to provide a possible field for active

* The other three were the *Mouvement de la Jeunesse Communiste* (MJC) for boys; the *Union des Jeunes Filles de France* (UJFF) for girls; and the *Union des Jeunes Agriculteurs de France* (UJAF) for peasants.

intervention. Leon Trotsky, whom the Stalinists thought they had buried, stalked again. It is no accident that French publishing houses should now be reissuing his works and selling them briskly to the undertwenties.

To be truly comprehensible, the student revolt which detonated this year's disturbances has to be traced back to the Algerian War. It was then that converged among young intellectuals the two currents of disillusion with the CPF and the impact of the colonial revolution. When historians come to draw up the balance sheet of the Algerian War, one of the cruelest colonial repressions in modern history, they will have to include the May Revolution among the longer-term consequences—on the debit or credit side, according to their politics.

At this point we must ask the reader to take a deep breath and bear with us. We are entering the jungle of proliferating clans and confusing initials.

French student organizations fall broadly into two categories: unions and political factions. The first are concerned, at least in theory, with the defense of specifically student interests; the second with political action on a wider stage than the university. The passions of the Algerian War brought into the public eye two such organizations, one of each sort: the Communist student youth organization, UEC, which we have already mentioned, and the *Union Nationale des Étudiants de France* (UNEF), the only French student union at the time.

The seven-year-long Algerian War, with its sorry record of brutality, torture, and miseries inflicted on a civilian population, deeply troubled the French conscience—and the tenderest conscience is the conscience of the young. As the agony dragged on, and successive French governments seemed powerless to check it, more and more young people began to play an active part in opposing it. They were drawn into running clandestine aid networks for the Al-

gerian National Liberation Front; they encouraged deser-
tions and insubordination inside the French armed forces;
many were inspired by the example of a professor called
Francis Jeanson, who played a leading role in such humane
resistance and was arrested in June, 1960. UNEF became
the principal channel for this student protest. Its passionate
opposition to the excesses of the war, the courage its young
members displayed, and its appeal to the principles of
French democracy forgotten in the heat of battle carried
the union into the forefront of French national politics. The
drive inside UNEF was provided by a core of left-wing
Catholics, moved as much by Christian charity as by
Marxist ideology. In those days they were as radical a body
of young people as one could find anywhere in France.
Indeed, their resistance to the war carried them to a position on the spectrum, way to the left of the French Communist Party which viewed them with ill-concealed distaste.

For the students the Algerian War was marked by two
great dates, two triumphs which they could claim as their
own. The first was an antiwar demonstration called by
UNEF on October 27, 1960, at the Place de la Bastille, in a
climate of anti-Arab racism and war hysteria. It was an
act of considerable political courage on the part of Pierre
Gaudez, UNEF's young president. At first the CPF and the
Communist-led trade union federation, the CGT, ruffled
by the student upstarts, ridiculed UNEF's bid to bring the
masses out. But after two weeks of negotiation they reluc-
tantly consented to take part. Then the government stepped
in and banned the demonstration. The CPF and CGT
climbed down, publicly renouncing "adventurism"; they
would bring out their men in small groups in suburban centers. But Gaudez stuck to his guns: The demonstration
would take place as planned.

It did take place—but at the Mutualité, a vast hall near
the Sorbonne, not at the Bastille, which was occupied by the
police—and was a great success, assembling some 10,000

people, an impressive figure for the time. (It was supported by the Catholic trade union federation, the CFDT, as well as by the ironworkers' section of the CGT, which had an old anarcho-syndicalist tradition.) It was UNEF's moment of glory and a key date for relations inside the French left. *L'Express,* the great standard-bearer for the protesting left during the Algerian War, featured UNEF and its prestigious president, Pierre Gaudez, on the front page. The CPF was discomfited.

But a revolt against the party was brewing nearer home, inside the CPF's own youth group, the UEC. From the late fifties part of the UEC rank and file became increasingly restive at the party's cautious, shilly-shallying attitude toward the war; it never robustly supported the cause of Algerian independence. These tensions came to a head in 1961, when the UEC, under the leadership of a group of students inspired by the positions of the Italian Communist Party, broke the CPF hold, acquiring virtual autonomy. Under this liberal "Italian" direction, the UEC enjoyed a spell of freethinking, unknown in the French Communist movement for decades.

The second great event in the students' history of the Algerian War was the creation, in April, 1961, of the *Front Universitaires Anti-Fasciste* (FUA), a fighting organization dedicated to the cause of Algerian independence, formed as a counter to the settlers' Secret Army Organization, the murderous OAS. The FUA brought together young left-wing militants of different coloring, but in particular a hard core from UNEF and UEC. Quickly the leaders gained the grass-roots support of several thousand schoolchildren and students. The Algerian War ended with the Évian agreements of March 19, 1962, followed from March to June by the unfolding of OAS terror in France. This period saw the FUA fully extended against the right. It was a delirious moment. The students discovered they were powerful. They enjoyed their first taste of direct action. They found they were capable of making a dent in adult politics without passing through the worn channels of the existing parties. This was a foretaste of the heady victories of May, 1968. A revolutionary leadership was in the making.

The return of peace brought anticlimax; it robbed UNEF of its glamor and of its national role. Tamely to demobilize its commandos was deeply frustrating. Inflamed with politics, UNEF's most active members could no longer really interest themselves in purely student grievances. The apolitical rank and file fell away, but the leaders were determined that the students' voice should continue to be heard in the adult world. The aftermath of the Algerian War, particularly the period from October, 1962, to January, 1963, marked an essential turning point in the nature of French student organizations. Here was the first conscious departure from the view that student unions need only concern themselves with the narrow defense of student interests. The new militants were groping toward a far more ambitious program, inspired by the challenging belief that students have a role to play in the shaping of society as a whole. But this function presupposes a radical transformation of the university itself. It was at this stage that all the themes later advanced in Berlin, Rome, and elsewhere were first tentatively sketched in: the struggle against the authoritarian caste-ridden university; the rejection of the university as servant of a technocratic society.

The student militants did not have it all their own way. They were a small avant-garde, and they ran into stiff opposition from the traditionalist majority—represented by an unholy alliance of the orthodox CPF and everything to the right of it. This majority was opposed to student unions moving into politics, urging that they should stick to university matters. For a year the battle raged back and forth in the Sorbonne, spilling out sometimes in street demonstrations. It was a battle not only between two abstract programs, but for the physical control of the union itself. It was not until September, 1963, that the Minos mustered their forces at a UNEF conference, outvoted the Majos and seized control. (The terms "Mino" and "Majo" were first introduced in 1956, when a left-wing Catholic minority clashed with a right-wing majority. The labels are still used today, although the Catholic element has given way to extremist Marxism and the Minos became the majority.)

The triumphant left-wing Minos established their head-quarters in the faculty of letters of the Sorbonne—or, to be more exact, in the faculty's UNEF subsection known as the *Fédération des Groupes d'Études de Lettres* (FGEL). It is to this militant subsection that one root of the May Revolution may be directly traced. FGEL became the nursery for avant-garde thinkers, providing many of the future leaders of UNEF in the revolutionary period then just opening—such men as Antoine Griset, Jean-Louis Peninou, and Marc Kravetz, who played a leading, behind-the-scenes role in the events of May, 1968. Meanwhile, the Majo traditionalists, beaten into retreat, dug themselves into the faculties of science, medicine, law, and political science. It was the free-ranging arts men—who included the sociologists—against the law-abiding sticklers of the liberal professions.

But there was a reverse side of the coin to the Minos triumph. UNEF virtually ceased to function as a union. It had never recovered the confidence of the authorities, outraged by its leap into politics during the Algerian War. Its official subsidy was cut and transferred instead to a tame "apolitical" government-sponsored creation called the FNEF (*Fédération Nationale des Étudiants de France*), which was a thorn in UNEF's flesh but never really got off the ground as an alternative union. FNEF's real role was to fight the spread of Marxist ideas in the university—at which it was singularly unsuccessful. Starved of funds, deprived of any really constructive role in the life of the university by the state's all-embracing hold, UNEF withered. In 1961 it had more than 100,000 members. By 1968 this

had fallen to around half that number, at a time when the
student population as a whole had soared from 240,000 to
more than 500,000. The name remained, the label, the
nationwide framework, but from 1966 to 1968 UNEF was
little more than a forum for rival political factions, each
eager to control it. In fact, it became scarcely distinguish-
able from the faction momentarily in the saddle. In the
provinces the local UNEF branches were often no more
than skeleton bodies, controlled by tiny militant caucuses,
constantly threatened with overthrow by a rival faction.
Power often changed hands several times in a single term.
These upsets in the provinces were a constant threat to the
Paris leadership, which, clinging precariously to power,
could not easily develop a coherent policy. This was
UNEF's situation when the revolution came to breathe new
life into it.

From 1966 onward the neat distinction we have so far
made between UNEF, the main student union, and UEC,
the only youth group worth mentioning on the left, no
longer covers the facts. We have seen the growth of a militant wing inside UNEF, seizing control of the union and
plunging it into politics, interested more in the nature of
society than in petty problems of libraries, student lodgings,
and holiday travel. This militant wing was not homogene-
ous. It was influenced, shaped, penetrated by extremist organizations spawned by UEC. Between 1966 and 1968 the
French Communist Party totally lost control of the most
active and militant elements in the student body. In this
period UEC's membership fell from an already derisory
4,000 to no more than around 1,500. It ceased to count.
Its place was taken by half a dozen clamorous sects, some
well structured, others the chaotic political expression
of surrealism. They include Trotskyists of all varieties,
Maoists, Guevarists, anarchists, "situationists" (whose main
contribution to the May Revolution were graffiti, joyful and

nonsensical). This sectarian flowering must not be dismissed as irrelevant; it provided not only the lunatic fringe, not only the bright colors, but also the hard core of determined leadership, the detonator of the earthquake which very nearly toppled General de Gaulle.

It will be recalled that, in the early 1960's, UEC was controlled by an "Italian" faction in dispute with the CPF. This situation could not last. In 1965 the CPF mounted an attack, expelled the "Italians," and regained control of its youth movement. But in the meantime, a militant element had grown up inside UEC, exactly parallel to the one in UNEF and springing from the same circumstances, the Algerian War and its aftermath. These militants soon clashed with the orthodox CPF leadership to face the fate of all Communist heretics—expulsion. The first purge came about as a result of a major policy decision by the Politburo of the French Communist Party, under Waldeck Rochet, who had taken over the leadership in 1964 from the ailing Maurice Thorez. Waldeck Rochet, more flexible than Thorez, swung the party into an electoral alliance with the Social Democrats—a pact symbolized by Communist support for the Socialist François Mitterrand at the French presidential elections of December, 1965. This alliance with the non-Communist left was fiercely contested by the young militants in the UEC. They wanted the party to be more, rather than less, revolutionary. They abhorred the prospect of a popular front, peaceful coexistence, indeed any compromise with the bourgeois world, nationally or internationally. They were kicked out.

A second charge against them was that they had helped found the *Comité Vietnam National* (CVN), with the slogan *FNL vaincra!* (The National Liberation Front will win). The CPF was furious. It saw in the new front, with its young leaders and galloping membership, a rival to its own peace movement, whose slogan—*Paix au Vietnam* (Peace in Vietnam)—now seemed tame. CPF support for

the Vietnam cause was made to appear halfhearted—as
the militants intended. A second purge got rid of the pro-
Chinese faction in the youth movement. The UEC was left
"pure" but bloodless.

What happened to all the troublesome militants who
were thrown out of the UEC? Where did they go? To answer this question is to outline the anatomy of revolutionary
politics on the French left. The victims of these UEC purges
wasted no time in getting organized. On April 2, 1966,
120 young men and women from sixteen French cities met
in Paris in a hall hung with portraits of Engels, Marx,
Lenin, Rosa Luxemburg, and Trotsky. This was the founding conference of the *Jeunesse Communiste Révolutionnaire* (JCR),* a tightly knit, well-disciplined Trotskyist
striking force, which emerged during the May Revolution
as perhaps the most formidable pressure group on the extreme left. From its creation to the great test in May, 1968,
the JCR has had just two years to get organized. It has no
ambition to be a mass party; rather its objective is to train
a hard core of revolutionary cadres, spread about the country at strategic points. The first secret target was believed
to have been a nucleus of 1,000 dedicated men. This target
has now been left far behind.

Much of the credit for this achievement belongs to a
cool-headed young man, Alain Krivine, the son of a well-to-
do French Jewish dentist. Krivine, now twenty-seven, was
a brilliant history student at the Sorbonne, and worked on
a history periodical published by Hachette until the aftermath of the May Revolution drove him underground. He
is a tall, dark young man, very calm and self-possessed. His
most striking qualities are relentless clarity, great fluency,
and the sort of realism rarely found in extremist politics. He

* Founder members include Alain Krivine, Henri Weber, and
Gérard Verbizier (from Paris) and Jean-Claude Laumonnier (from
Rouen), all still on the seven-man *Bureau National*. Second-gener-
ation leaders include Xavier Langlade, Daniel Bensaid, and Jean-
François Godchau (from Nanterre).

is married to the daughter of the left-wing writer and politician Gilles Martinet. Krivine started his political life in the CPF's youth group, the UEC, but like so many others, he edged away from orthodox Communism during the Algerian War.

Inevitably the JCR structure and internal organization resemble those of the Communist youth movements in which its militants grew up. Consciously, its founders modeled themselves on the youth movements of Lenin's Bolshevik Party. The basic JCR unit is the circle. Full membership is granted only after a period—a minimum of three months —of observer status, during which time the new recruit must win his spurs. He must not only understand JCR doctrines, but be skillful at defending them. He must be a propagandist and missionary. To us, at least in our contacts with the organization, it has appeared that the JCR is careful to recruit young people of high intelligence and engaging personality. Discipline is strict, but the accent is on self-discipline. An errant member may find himself censured by his circle, demoted to observer status, or even, for grave breaches, expelled (although the JCR explains that any such expulsion would, of course, follow "democratic" discussion and not in any way resemble a "bureaucratic" purge!).

The first article of faith of the JCR, borrowed from their patron saint Trotsky, is the need to create an avant-garde revolutionary leadership in France. Without such a leadership, there can be no effective mass revolutionary party, and without a mass party, no seizure of power. It need hardly be said that these young Trotskyists consider the French Communist Party to have failed hopelessly in this task; for them it is ossified, caste-ridden, frozen in sterile bureaucracy. Worse still, it has become no more than a left-wing Social Democratic Party, courting bourgeois alliances, dreaming of parliamentary respectability, wrapping itself piously in the Tricolor. The slump in revolutionary

fervor of the CPF reflects that of the Soviet Union, itself
in the grip of a nonrevolutionary bureaucracy. This disastrous situation must be corrected. The JCR recognizes that
the mass of the French working class still remains faithful,
in its innocence, to the Communist Party. It cannot be
weaned away by noisy propaganda directed against this
powerful monolith from the outside. Agitation must be carried on *inside* the CPF and *inside* its dependent trade union
federation, the CGT, to detach from the Communist corpse
whole sections of the working class and restore them to
their revolutionary vocation.

By revolution the JCR means something pretty specific:
clashes in factories and in the street; a trial of strength outside Parliament; the violent capture of state power. "The
question of whether this contest is bloody will depend not
on the proletariat, but on the bourgeoisie," JCR propagan-
dists assert. "In any event the working class must be ready
for armed combat." The events of May in France come as
a reminder that such a prospect is not entirely unimagina-
ble.

The JCR's violent philosophy closely resembles that of
the *Parti Communiste Internationaliste* (PCI), the French
branch of the Trotskyist Fourth International, an organization rent by schisms and greatly weakened by twenty-five
years of Stalinist repression, but which has perked up since
the rash of student revolts around the world. Both the JCR
and the PCI have a special affection for Cuba. The Fourth
International is not a secret society or a disciplined monolith, like its far more prosperous orthodox Communist
cousin. It is run from shabby offices in Paris, Brussels, and
Rome, by a three-man unified secretariat: Pierre Frank
(France), Ernest Mandel (Belgium), and Livio Maitan
(Italy). Frank is a short, kindly, unaffected man, with the
quiet passion of a lifelong revolutionary. He was Trotsky's
secretary in Turkey in 1929 and is today a main source of
ideological wisdom for the young militants of the JCR. No

direct organizational links bind the JCR to the PCI, but
the founders and leaders of the youth group tend to be
members of the parent body. The JCR publishes *Avant-
garde Jeunesse,* a monthly containing JCR news from the
provinces, blood and thunder from Vietnam, inspiration
from Cuba, and a solid diet of ideological indoctrination.
More theoretical material is provided by the PCI in its
monthly and especially in its quarterly journal—both called
La Quatrième Internationale.

The JCR is not alone in waving the Trotskyist banner.
It has a fierce rival in the *Fédération des Étudiants Révolutionnaires* (FER),* a combative, ultrasectarian Trotskyist
sect, which makes the JCR seem mild and reasonable. The
FER grew out of the CLER *(Comité de Liaison des Étudiants Révolutionnaires),* an earlier faction, dating back to
October, 1961, the result of a split in 1953 between Pierre
Frank and Pierre Lambert inside the French branch of the
Fourth International.† The *Lambertistes* pride themselves
on the most intransigent Bolshevism and the strictest doctrinal purity. As we have seen, the JCR is reasonably pragmatic in its relations with the hated CPF, arguing that this
fortress can be captured only from the inside. The FER
rejects such deviousness, maintaining that priority must be
given to building up a revolutionary organization around
itself, sole possessor of holy writ. In appearance, members
of FER seem more military than political. They admire
strong-arm methods, they are often armed, they have a
quite alarming fanatical look in the eye, and their harangues
tend to be delivered with the tempo and violence of ma-
chine-gun fire. They are indifferent to unpopularity, as men
confident in their own righteousness. Their organ is a
monthly called *Révoltes.*

Yet another small Marxist faction is the *Union Commu-*

* Its leading personalities are Claude Chisseray and Charles Berg.
† As a result of the split, the *Organisation Communiste Inter-
nationaliste* (OCI) was founded. Now run by Pierre Lambert and
Stephan Just, it publishes *Information Ouvrière.*

niste, better known under the name of its newspaper, *Voix Ouvrière.* It enjoys the distinction of being the oldest Trotskyist splinter group, and the one with the best claim to have some worker support. It is not, however, affiliated with the Fourth International.*

A noticeably different political development was that of the pro-Chinese militants, who, after being purged from the UEC, founded in November, 1966, the *Union des Jeunesses Communistes (Marxistes-Léninistes)* (UJC[M-L]).†
In numbers and determination, they are in the same league as the JCR, but their strategy is different. From the start they focused their activity not on the university, but on the factory. Their attitude is one of humble devotion to the working class, and their slogan (as well as the name of their party organ) is *Servir le Peuple.* Some dozen of their militants have given up their studies to work in factories. They are a Maoist equivalent to the worker-priest. Their intensely serious high-mindedness makes them wholly unlike the rebellious children of well-off parents, caricatured by Jean-Luc Godard in *La Chinoise* as wearing smart Mao tunics and brandishing little red books. There is, of course, a touch of unbalanced fanaticism in their praise of the thought of Chairman Mao and in their fierce attacks against the bureaucrats of the Communist-led trade unions. They insult the Communist Party by referring to it with scathing quotation marks as the P "C" F or as the PCF(R)—*R* standing for revisionist, the last word in infamy. But while others talked of the working class and of the need to bridge the gap between intellectual and manual workers, the UJC (M-L) members, with their quiet single-mindedness, were already inside the factory gates. Their role in the May

* On May 19, 1968, the PCI, JCR, *Voix Ouvrière,* and another Trotskyist circle called *Groupes Marxistes Révolutionnaires* agreed to a joint link in the form of a coordination committee.
† Many of its founding members were graduates of the École Normale Supérieure, where they had fallen under the influence of the Maoist thinker Professor Louis Althusser. The movement's leading figure is the "theoretician" Robert Linhart.

Revolution was not of the first rank; as we shall see, they did not wholly lend their support to the strategy of Daniel Cohn-Bendit and the JCR. But in May they did widen their enclaves inside working-class territory, in the form of a number of *Comités de Soutien au Luttes du Peuple*.

The UJC(M-L) has no close link with the PCMLF *(Parti Communiste Marxiste-Léniniste de France),** founded by pro-Chinese Communists on December 31, 1967, after they had been expelled from the French Communist Party. The PCMLF publishes *L'Humanité Nouvelle* and sees itself as a truly revolutionary party, as opposed to the revisionist CPF. This move was frowned upon by the well-drilled young theorists of the UJC(M-L), who considered the formation of the party untimely.

Much of this revolutionary fervor on the left of the Communist Party has been powered by one major issue: the Vietnam War. As a prodder of tender consciences, as a mobilizer of radical sympathies, it has far outstripped even the Algerian War. No youth group has made more successful use of it than the JCR. Thanks to the Vietnam War, the JCR and, to a lesser extent, its rivals have managed to make contact with thousands of young people, in schools and universities. French government policy itself played into their hands by sensitizing young consciences to the war. Frequently over the last couple of years the French state television service has shown horror pictures from Vietnam, many of them North Vietnamese propaganda films. Perhaps to justify its anti-American policy, the Gaullist regime overplayed the theme of violence in Vietnam. Many young people were traumatized by what they saw on the screen. "I can't bear it anymore," said a fifteen-year-old boy who shuddered and switched off his set.

In the autumn of 1966 the JCR and its allies, notably some Castroists and the *Parti Socialiste Unifié* (PSU), a left-wing breakaway Socialist group, set up a Vietnam

* Gilbert Mury is its best-known member.

front organization as a means of reaching a wider public. It was called the *Comité Vietnam National* (CVN)* and itself spawned scores of regional committees, drawing into the protest movement many who had no particular knowledge of, or sympathy for, the politics of the founders. Distinguished personalities, such as the mathematician Laurent Schwartz, lent their names. Schoolchildren—already restive at the strict discipline, the old-fashioned curricula, the learning by rote, the grim, barrackslike *lycées*—proved fertile ground for anti-American, anti-Vietnam agitation. A litter of CVN committees sprang up in the schools and, in spite of headmasters' opposition, proved so successful that late in 1967 it was decided to mobilize schoolchildren still more energetically for left-wing political action. The vehicle chosen was a network of school-based committees called *Comités d'Action Lycéens* (CAL's),† deliberately loosely structured and nonsectarian to draw in the crowds. Schoolchildren joined by the thousands.

The CAL's played a vital, if unsung, role in drumming up the rabble armies which so effectively harassed the police during the May Revolution.

The CAL militants—often long-haired revolutionary romantics, very different in style from the soberly dressed members of the CPF youth groups—soon made life hell for their teachers. Their slogan was, Freedom of action in school!—by which they meant agitation, distributing tracts, boycotting classes, disrupting exams. In their minds they often equated class struggle with struggle in class. There are precedents in recent French history for teen-age political involvement: The Germans shot five Paris schoolboys from the Lycée Buffon for Resistance activities during the war, and left-wing schoolboys fought the OAS in the streets of

* The *Bureau National* of the CVN includes such left-wing militants as the Castroists Jean-Pierre Vigier and Jean Schalit, the JCR leader Alain Krivine, Denis Berger, and others.

† Michel Recanati, a seventeen-year-old schoolboy (born in September, 1950), is one of the most remarkable of these teen-age politicians.

Paris in 1962. In May, 1968, it was the CAL's that sabotaged the baccalaureate, that cornerstone of the whole French educational system. Like their elder brothers and sisters in the embattled Sorbonne, they fought for the same rights: freedom to run their own affairs; freedom to have their say; freedom to work at politics; freedom to make love. "We want the Pill," the teen-agers clamored. "We want a normal sex life at seventeen."

Student extremists detonated the May Revolution. These young politicians came, as we have seen, from two nurseries—UNEF and the UEC—student bodies deeply shaken not only by internal French developments (such as the demographic boom cracking the seams of an old-fashioned university), but also by stirring events farther afield: the Algerian War; Cuba; Vietnam; the creeping paralysis which seemed to overtake Soviet Communism. The result of this ferment was the forging of a revolutionary pressure group on the extreme left, whose existence was as much a threat to the French Communist Party as to the French bourgeois state. How everyone from left to right ganged up to crush the young troublemakers is one of the principal themes of this book.

3 Takeoff

EVERY country in the world with troublesome students now asks itself the question: Could it happen here? None can feel complacent. Of course, revolutions are not caused only by revolutionaries; there must also be a revolutionary situation which they recognize and exploit. The detonator can only work if there is enough tinder lying about. But no one should underestimate the intelligence, audacity, and sheer strategic skill of the student leaders who, in cafés and on university campuses around the world, are planning to give the adults hell. In France this phenomenon was particularly striking; the detonator was of high quality.

The May Revolution was led by a coalition: different backgrounds, talents, political experience; different sorts of men. This was its strength. The voice of the movement —and what a voice!—was that of Daniel Cohn-Bendit, then a twenty-three-year-old second-year sociology student at Nanterre—a brilliant student, according to his professor, the sixty-two-year-old Marxist philosopher Henri Lefebvre. Cohn-Bendit had a serious part to play in triggering the revolutionary avalanche, but he is mainly remembered for stamping the student revolt with his special brand of impudent clowning. He turned clowning into a punishing political weapon. Totally unimpressed by age, rank, or authority—by all the protective cant of the adult world— his talent was to keep a mocking finger pointed at the emperor's testicles. With breathtaking cheekiness he stripped the clothes from the stuffy university authorities, the hard-boiled police, from the *roi soleil* himself in the Élysée Palace. His threat to make a repeat performance from London of De Gaulle's celebrated June 18, 1940, broadcast to occupied France, was a stroke of irreverent PR genius.

Cohn-Bendit has the jester's gift for repartee, for improvisation, for popping up inside his opponent's guard. Banned from France, with dozens of police mobilized on the German frontier to keep him out, he bounced up like an infernal jack-in-the-box in the heart of Paris, his flaming hair dyed an unconvincing black. It was a stroke of drama, more farcical than heroic, but politically masterly. Without his cocky, elastic smile, the revolution would have seemed sinister. He disarmed the public and made the vast, steel-helmeted police machine mobilized against the students seem grotesque. He is a Brigitte Bardot of politics, perfect of his type, brazen, holding all eyes. But his role is not all glamor and mischief. He proved in Nanterre to be a great mobilizer of uncommitted opinion. His magnetism drew men to him. But second, he was also a channel, perhaps the most important one, for the spread to France of ideas and techniques of student militancy which the SDS (*Sozialistischer Deutscher Studentenbund*) had developed in German universities.

The SDS president, Karl Dietrich Wolff, a stripling of twenty-five who looks eighteen, came to Nanterre to lend a hand at a crucial moment in April, the month before the revolution's takeoff. The SDS believes that student uprisings have a role to play in the worldwide class struggle; that from their university base, transformed into a model of the democratic society of the future, students can expose the repressive nature of modern capitalism and its production-line conception of man as a "specialized idiot." In France, as in Germany, the revolutionaries sought from the start to create in both universities and factories genuinely democratic students' and workers' councils—rival institutions to those of the bourgeois state. What was specifically new about this challenge was less its ideas than its shock tactics. Agitation, harassment, provocation, systematic indiscipline, both physical and intellectual—everything that is summed up in the French phrase *contestation permanente*—this was the sharp instrument that punctured the balloon of De Gaulle's complacent, monolithic state. In Nanterre intimidation sometimes took a primitive form: "Say death to the Americans in Vietnam, or I'll box your ears" was one girl's introduction to the March 22 Movement.

But there is yet another strand in Cohn-Bendit's political persona: anarchism, a spirit which flourished in the idle, pointless vacuum of Nanterre, rather than at the more socially rooted Sorbonne. Cohn-Bendit's political allies often describe him, in private and with some irritation, as *inorganisé et inorganisable* (disorganized and beyond organization). It was this quality of undefined, surging spontaneity which he contributed to his March 22 Movement. He always refused the title of leader, preferring that of spokesman. The movement, he said tirelessly, had no organization, no structure, no hierarchy, no hard-and-fast program.

At the heart of this moving mass was a handful of activists, like a pebble in a snowball. They gave the first push, and now and then an occasional directional shove, but could no more check the headlong course than a canoeist in the rapids. This wild élan left a trail of nonsense graffiti on the walls of Nanterre, Paris, and every other faculty of France, spreading like a laughing disease to the metro. *"Violez votre Alma Mater,"* an anonymous scribbler wrote in Nanterre, birthplace of the March 22 Movement. Other lines in this long, scattered political poem were *"Je suis marxiste tendance Groucho"* and *"L'anarchie c'est je."**

* "Rape your Alma mater"; "I'm a Marxist of the Groucho faction"; "Anarchy is I." These and other slogans in this book appear in a remarkable collection by Julien Besançon, *Les Murs Ont la Parole* (Paris, Claude Tchou, 1968).

In retrospect, it was this streak of fertile, creative anarchy which Cohn-Bendit carried into political action.

He was "the redhead without a country, the democrat of the street, carrying within him anarchism and Marxism, joining the two flags, the black and the red, whose coupling was the symbol of the student revolt." *

The *Jeunesse Communiste Révolutionnaire* (JCR) † was the first political faction to recognize Cohn-Bendit's potential for revolutionary struggle and to join forces with him. Strongly implanted in Nanterre, it was thus a founder element in the March 22 Movement, part of that *minorité agissante* (activist minority) at the core of the snowball. But there could be no greater contrast between the disciplined, purposeful JCR cadres and the freebooting Cohn-Bendit. The JCR penetrated his movement, melting unobtrusively into it, in accordance with its avowed *entriste* philosophy. (This was a principle the Trotskyists evolved in their struggle with the French Communist Party; they could not credibly set themselves up as a rival *party* to the big brother, but planned instead to enter the CPF and subvert it from the inside.) The JCR won the confidence of Cohn-Bendit and his friends by not seeking to take over the movement or manipulate it to its own exclusive ends; instead, it gave the March 22 unconditional support. In this way, the JCR became Cohn-Bendit's principal ally, stiffening his anarchism with Leninist political intelligence.

The other Trotskyist faction, the *Fédération des Étudiants Révolutionnaires* (FER).†† was less successful. Its belief in its own revolutionary vocation prevented this sort of flexible compromise. It was, moreover, kept at arm's length by the JCR. Failing to get in at the start, the FER

---

* "*Le rouquin sans patrie, le démocrat de la rue, portant en lui anarchisme et marxisme, mêlant les deux drapeaux, dont l'accouplement est le symbole de la révolte étudiante, le noir est le symbole de la révolte étudiante, le noir et le rouge.*" Edgar Morin, *Le Monde* (June 5, 1968).

† See page 49.

†† See page 52.

had little influence on the later course of the revolution. In contrast, the pro-Chinese *Union des Jeunesses Communistes (Marxistes-Léninistes)* (UJC[M-L])* began by denouncing Cohn-Bendit's movement as reactionary, but in April, shortly before takeoff, it changed its mind and publicly confessed its error before an audience of 800 students: "We had preconceived sectarian ideas about student movements because they so rarely succeed," the UJC(M-L) representative said. "But we have now decided to merge with the March 22 like fish in water." There was thunderous applause—and the UJC(M-L) was in, to play a role second only to that of the JCR in the events of May. When the revolt spread to the workers, the UJC(M-L)'s philosophy of *Servir le Peuple* at last seemed justified. It is perhaps no accident that the only death on the students' side during the revolt should be that of a UJC(M-L) schoolboy militant, drowned in the Seine on June 10 near the Renault works at Flins, fleeing before a police charge.

By the last week of March, 1968, Cohn-Bendit and his Nanterre movement were making headlines in the French press, but in that same week, away from the spotlight, powerful support for his revolt was being mobilized in Paris. Readers of the chapter on Latin Quarter politics will remember that one of the springs of the May Revolution was a radical current which had grown up since the Algerian War in the arts section of the students' union, UNEF. Militants of this arts section, known as the FGEL (*Fédération des Groupes D'Études de Lettres*), recognized in Cohn-Bendit's ideas an echo of the themes they had been advancing as far back as 1963. They had been the first coherent critics of the French university, the first to want to bring down the old structure. Now, in late March, 1968, the climate seemed ripe for action. In early March these militants formed the *Mouvement d'Action Universitaire* (MAU) and on the twenty-ninth held their first public

* See page 53.

meeting in the Richelieu Amphitheater at the Sorbonne. They grabbed the lecture hall against the will of the authorities, who had forbidden the meeting—perhaps the first time such a thing had happened in the history of the old Sorbonne. It was a revolutionary act. The police gathered outside but did not intervene.

The MAU militants were unlike either the rambunctious Cohn-Bendit or the disciplined politicos of the JCR and UJC(M-L). For one thing MAU men were older, mostly graduate students and research workers in their middle and late twenties already half-integrated into the society they criticized. Many were veterans of student protest during the Algerian War. They were clever, politically experienced, mature; they represented a Sorbonne Marxist elite, unaffiliated with any party, high-minded, humane. They brought to the revolution a moral and intellectual weight which, at a crucial moment on May 3, helped swing the great mass of the student and teaching bodies behind the *enragés*.

These, then, were the principal forces which came together to form the leadership of the student revolt: the March 22 Movement; the JCR; the UJC(M-L); and the MAU. They were soon joined by the schoolboy army of the *Comités d'Action Lycéens* (CAL's)* and by the leaders of the *Comité Vietnam National* (CVN),† the left-wing anti-Vietnam War front organization. From late April or early May a secret high command of the revolution started meeting regularly or stayed in close touch by telephone and courier. It included Daniel Cohn-Bendit, twenty-three; Alain Krivine, twenty-seven, of JCR; Marc Kravetz, twenty-six, and Jean-Louis Peninou, twenty-six, of MAU; Michel Recanati, seventeen, of CAL; and Jean-Pierre Vigier, forty, of CVN. Two other leaders soon joined this high command and leaped to public prominence, more

* See page 55.
† See page 55.

by being caught in the eye of the television cameras than because of the troops they could muster. They were Jacques Sauvageot, twenty-five, the wildly handsome vice-president of the withered UNEF, which, under the pressure of events, became a convenient umbrella for the revolutionary movement as a whole, and the plump Alain Geismar, twenty-nine, national secretary of the university teachers' union, SNESup (*Syndicat National de l'Enseignement Supérieure*).*

It would be a mistake to consider this command a tightly knit revolutionary apparatus. It was not. These men were agreed on long-term political objectives, rather than on immediate tactics. They were held together by ideology, not by organization or planning. This gave them the guerrilla-like flexibility to hold their own against the state in the insurrection which was about to burst upon them and unfold at breakneck speed.

The May, 1968, explosion was foreshadowed by an ugly rash of petty guerrilla attacks in the Latin Quarter and in some outlying universities. In Nanterre itself, at the start of the new term after the Easter holidays, there were ominous developments. The *enragés* declared their intention to boycott the sacrosanct exams—symbol of the university's subservience to the social hierarchies and career system of adult life. They would have nothing to do with these initiation rites into modern society. The dean was foolish enough to retort that the exams would be held at all costs, under police protection if necessary. The *enragés* were

* SNESup is one of three unions which make up the FEN, *Fédération de l'Éducation Nationale*. FEN, uniting left-wing teachers from radicals to the Communist Party, was historically the champion of the *école laïque*, removed from clerical influence. The other two unions inside FEN are the SNI (*Syndicat National des Instituteurs*), the big primary school teachers' union, and the SNES (*Syndicat National de l'Enseignement du Second Degré*) for secondary school teachers. SNESup's conservative rival is the *Autonome* (*Syndicat Autonome de l'Enseignement Supérieure*), the chief pressure group of the intellectual establishment.

delighted: What could point more clearly to the oppressive role of the university than exams held under police supervision? At their wits' end, the teaching staff split into hawks and doves. The more numerous hawks recommended firmness and the recruitment of a campus police force, responsible to the director. The liberal doves, while deploring the *enragés'* insolent tactics, argued that clamping down would not pay and that the only remedy was frank discussion with the students. On April 23 Cohn-Bendit was taken for questioning to the Nanterre police station after a right-wing student had been wounded in a brawl, and criminal proceedings were opened against him.

At Toulouse University on April 25 the police had to intervene for the first time in thirty years to separate warring bands of left- and right-wing students. On the same day in Nanterre a member of the CPF Central Committee, Pierre Juquin, invited to give a lecture, was driven violently from the podium by a UJC(M-L) commando. Three days later a CVN force, helmeted and armed with iron bars, mounted a fierce punitive expedition against a pro-South Vietnam exhibition in St.-Germain-des-Prés. Dean Grappin of Nanterre had tried to stem the tide before the Easter holidays by closing the faculty for a couple of days and by putting a lecture room at the disposal of the turbulent politicos. They took it, renamed it *Amphi Che Guevara,* but added unappeased: "We don't need any such little gifts. We'll take what buildings we need, when we need them."

Although the student left now seemed the more combative, it was in fact right-wing students who had kept alive a mood of violence in the Latin Quarter since the end of the Algerian War. Their tactics were intimidation. No more than a few hundred, they were grouped in two organizations: the *Fédération des Étudiants Nationalistes* and the paramilitary *Occident,* one of whose heroes is the right-wing lawyer and politician Maître Tixier-Vignancour. On

Thursday, May 2, an *Occident* commando raided the Sorbonne headquarters of the FGEL, home base of the MAU. They set the room afire, tore out the telephone, and marked the chimney piece with their sign, a cross inside a circle. The right was preparing for battle. That very morning an editorial in *Minute,* a right-wing scandal sheet, had declared: "Cohn-Bendit should be taken to the frontier by the scruff of his neck. . . . And if the authorities don't feel up to it, we know a number of young Frenchmen who are itching to carry out this public cleansing operation."

At Nanterre, too, Thursday was an eventful day. A group of 300 *enragés* seized a lecture hall and proceeded to show a film on the life of Che Guevara, ignoring the appeals of a history professor who was due to give a lecture there. A guard commando, armed with slings and stones, stood ready in the event of an attack by *Occident,* which had threatened to come in strength "to crush the Marxists." That evening Dean Grappin, shattered by what he described as "an intolerable mood, a real war psychosis," decided once more to close the faculty, this time for an unlimited period. Before the day was out, it was learned that Cohn-Bendit and five of his friends had been summoned to appear on May 6 before the diciplinary council of the University of Paris. The charge was not made public, but it was thought to include harassing students and insults to staff. The MAU sprang to his defense in a tract: "Of course, lecturers, eminent professors, have been insulted, criticized and routed. . . . But since when have you mandarins deserved the students' confidence? You are supposed to be teachers, but you are no more than pompous pillars of a bourgeois university. . . ."

That Thursday morning, May 2, with the heavens about to open, Georges Pompidou, the Prime Minister, and his Foreign Minister, Maurice Couve de Murville, accompanied by their wives, left Orly for the long flight to Teheran, on the first leg of an official ten-day visit to Iran and Af-

ghanistan. The absence of M. Pompidou robbed the French
government of the one man who might have been able to
check the tide of insurrection before it got out of hand.
He alone among the ministers had wrested from President
de Gaulle a certain measure of real executive authority. At
the time of his departure he was beginning to behave like
a real Prime Minister, not just a servant of the court. When
the student revolt took off on May 3, the President did not
act—student brawls were too petty an issue to engage his
personal intervention—whereas the man Pompidou left
behind to replace him in his absence, Louis Joxe, the Acting Premier, lacked the authority to impose on his Cabinet
colleagues his own liberal sentiments. For ten days, then,
as the revolt gathered pace, the French government
fumbled.

Shortly after lunch on Friday, May 3, as the afternoon's
lectures were beginning, some 500 angry left-wing students
gathered in the great paved central courtyard of the Sorbonne. They were there to protest against the closure by
Dean Grappin of the Nanterre faculty of letters and more
particularly against the summons to six Nanterre *enragés,*
including Cohn-Bendit, to appear on Monday before the
university's disciplinary council. Harangued by their leaders from the chapel steps, the Sorbonne protestors were
hard-core political cadres. Here was the revolutionary high
command, surrounded by its handpicked militants. Most of
the key movements were represented: student spokesmen
from UNEF; the JCR under its leader, Alain Krivine; the
ultrasectarian Trotskyist fanatics of the FER; a strong
March 22 contingent from Nanterre led by Cohn-Bendit;
and, from the Sorbonne itself, the graduate political veterans of the MAU, whose premises had been sacked the day
before by young thugs from *Occident.* An *Occident* commando was thought to be still roaming the Latin Quarter,
looking for trouble, and the left-wingers in the Sorbonne

had formed their own militia, or *service d'ordre*, armed with sticks and iron bars. (In the violent climate of Latin Quarter politics, each faction recruits among its members a few toughs to form a *service d'ordre*, or SO as the students call it; fisticuffs are a natural extension of student politics. At moments of crisis the SO's are swollen by on-the-spot *ad hoc* recruitment.)

To the anxious university authorities, the meeting was beginning to look nasty. If *Occident* chose to attack, to "clean out the place" as it had threatened, there was a real danger that the Sorbonne would become a battlefield. Students were massing in the Boulevard St.-Michel and in the Place de la Sorbonne, the little square overhung by the dome of the university. Police reinforcements had been called up on the approach roads to contain the crowds. Jean Roche, rector of the University of Paris, started to worry.

In normal times Roche is a cool-headed distinguished biochemist, a highly intelligent product of rather straitlaced upper-middle-class France. He found the noisy turbulent leftists profoundly distasteful. A day or two earlier he had gone down to take a look at Nanterre and had seen for himself just how disruptive a handful of *enragés* could be. He had been shocked by their decision to sabotage the exams, which to anyone brought up in the French system was like an offense against Holy Writ. He was deeply perturbed at the thought of the virus spreading to the teeming ant heap of student Paris, already tense and restive in the cramped and creaking university structure.

Telephoning for advice to the Minister of Education, he agreed with Alain Peyrefitte that the increasingly stormy gathering in the Sorbonne must be broken up and the courtyard cleared. But the *enragés* had already refused repeated appeals from university officials to end their meeting and disperse. Some had broken up furniture to arm themselves with chair legs. As Roche and Peyrefitte saw it that after-

noon, the police would have to be called in. No one is sure
which of the two men bears the prime responsibility for
that fateful decision. Roche at least signed the written au-
thorization to allow the police into the hitherto sacrosanct
precinct of the university. But people who know Roche
claim he would not have called for police help without
pressure from the minister. Peyrefitte, a former diplomat,
showed little diplomatic skill. By resorting immediately to
force, he left himself with no freedom of maneuver and
led the government up a blind alley.

At about 4:45 P.M. a strong column of helmeted police,
armed with hardened rubber truncheons and shields,
marched through the narrow arched entrance into the courtyard and surrounded the demonstrators. There was hardly
a scuffle. The students offered no resistance and agreed to
leave after talks between Alain Krivine of the JCR and
other student leaders and Roger Grosperrin, assistant director of the Paris prefecture. Step by step the police cordon
pressed the mass of students back toward the entrance,
where, in groups of twenty-five or so, they were bundled,
boys and girls together, into black, shuttered trucks, parked
close to the walls of the university and blocking the Rue
de la Sorbonne.

A hush fell over the street. Some daring students pushed
forward to see what was happening to their comrades, who
could be glimpsed, packed tight on wooden benches,
through the wire-mesh windows of the police vans. Silent
with shock, the young spectators watched the great black
mass of armed police, a sinister invading army with goggled
outriders like the emissaries of death in Jean Cocteau's
Orphée. Something horrible and ugly was happening.

As the first police van with its sullen load left the gate
of the Sorbonne to turn into the little *place,* a wave of outrage swept over the waiting crowd. There were jeers and
shouts, scattered at first then swelling into great rhythmic
chants of À BAS LA RÉPRESSION! Suddenly there was a

sharp movement. Someone threw a stone, then another. A windshield was shattered, and the police driver had blood streaming down his face. Surging up to the vans, the students pounded with their fists against the metal flanks. Others lifted parked cars onto the road to block the van. The first, sketchy barricade was up. Then came the exploding plop of a gas grenade, and then another, and clouds of acrid smoke swirled up from the sidewalks, driving screaming, weeping students into cafés and doorways and out of the *place* into the boulevard. A car was trapped in the crowd. Two young men leaped onto the hood and yelled out battle orders.

These first few minutes of the insurrection set a pattern which was to be tragically repeated throughout the month. The authorities had blundered badly by penetrating the Sorbonne, and taking into custody scores of young people whose only offense had been to make a little noise. They had then compounded the error by parading their prisoners in front of their comrades. As was so often to happen, repression bred violence, rather than stifled it. The immediate effect of the authorities' crude display of strength was to unite the mass of uncommitted students—and their teachers—behind the *enragés*. In a few minutes a mass movement was created. Combat in the street, the simple act of reaching for a stone and throwing it at a police officer, the lightning solidarity bred in a fighting crowd—this was the instant political education which turned the student population, from one moment to the next, into an army of rebels.

All that evening police and demonstrators ebbed and flowed up and down the boulevards of the Latin Quarter, dancers in a grotesque ballet. The students lit fires on the roads, melting the tar and loosening the cobblestones, which they hurled at their enemies. Iron gratings from around the trees on the sidewalks were torn up. Traffic signs were thrown onto the roadway to check the police charges. The urge to fight, to clobber, to draw blood, spread like a raging epidemic. Stung to fury by the flying stones, the police laid about them wildly with their truncheons, hitting innocent and guilty with equal ferocity. Commuters, emerging unaware onto the battlefield from metro stations, were felled. Sidewalk cafés were stormed and tables overturned. Simple passersby were rounded up ferociously and trundled away in police vans. Everywhere clouds of tear gas made the air unbreathable. By the end of the day hundreds were wounded, and 596 people were in custody, including Jacques Sauvageot, the UNEF leader, and Daniel Cohn-Bendit, who was held for twenty-four hours. That weekend four young men were sent to prison for two months. The students had a new slogan: *Libérez nos camarades!* Thoroughly shaken, Rector Roche closed the Sorbonne until further notice. To protest against this lockout, UNEF called on the 160,000 students of the Paris region to demonstrate on Monday, the day Cohn-Bendit was due to appear before the disciplinary council. SNESup called for a teachers' strike. It was war. The revolution had begun. That same day, May 3, 1968, Paris was chosen as the site for the Vietnam peace talks.

4   Winning the Street Battle

STUDENTS are far better equipped for insurrection than most adults recognize. They have time to plot; freedom from bread-and-butter constraints; the confidence of their class and education; faculty buildings in which to meet; above all, *energy*—the energy to march from one end of Paris to the other, to fight all night, and still be fit enough to draft, print, and distribute a revolutionary tract before dawn. Adults are no match for such demonic staminas.

In the week from Monday, May 6, to Monday, May 13, the students' revolt changed fundamentally in character: From pranks and street brawls it became a mass insurrection. In that week the revolutionary leaders first took command—however tenuously—of large-scale forces and demonstrated their gifts for mobile strategy, spreading disorder across the face of Paris and tying down tens of thousands of police. The revolutionaries set the pace; they seized the initiative, forcing a baffled government into error after error. Within the first twenty-four hours the movement spread to provincial universities, provoking a rash of demonstrations and strikes at Aix-en-Provence, Bordeaux, Caen, Clermont-Ferrand, Dijon, Grenoble, Montpellier, Nantes, Rouen, and Toulouse. In that first unforgettable week the most striking quality of the student explosion was joy. Later the revolt was to degenerate into pathos and squalor, but at this early stage, whatever the cold plotting of some of the leaders, it all seemed wild youthful exhilaration, full of a crazy utopian hope. There was a spontaneous surge of the spirit, expressed in the marvelous claim scrawled on the faculty wall: "Here imagination rules!" The most cynical adults were moved. Public sympathy welled up, enclosing the rebels in a protective cocoon so that they became invulnerable. The authorities only blackened themselves by striking at them.

Seething from the police "rape" of the Sorbonne on Friday and from the weekend sentences imposed on four young men, 4,000 to 5,000 student demonstrators responded to the call of Jacques Sauvageot, the UNEF leader, to turn out at 9 A.M. on Monday morning. But nothing much happened before lunch, except for a spirited march around the Latin Quarter, marked by small clashes with the police and the chanting of new slogans: "Roche resign!" "Professors not cops!" Cohn-Bendit was otherwise occupied. Singing the "Internationale" and with clenched fists raised, he and the other Nanterre troublemakers, accompanied by their lawyer, reported early that morning at the Sorbonne for their "trial" by the university's disciplinary council. The ushers wanted them in one at a time. They refused, saying they would go in together or not at all. The authorities gave way. The council—the seven deans of the Paris faculties, supported by two jurists—sat until 1 P.M. The meeting was lively. "We had four hours of fun," Cohn-Bendit said laconically as he left the Sorbonne to join the daylong demonstration in the street.

There was no checking the headlong flight of events. For the first time since the Algerian War, dozens of university teachers marched with the students. Support came also from hundreds of teen-age militants, mobilized for the occasion by the school action committees, the CAL's. A procession formed after lunch outside the new science faculty on the Quai St.-Bernard, and headed toward Notre Dame along the river, growing all the time and derisively chanting: *Nous sommes un groupuscule"* (We are a tiny group)—a reference to the many critics, on the conservative right as in the orthodox Communist Party, who sneeringly dismissed the student protest as the work of a handful of trouble-makers. Nowhere along their route, as the marchers turned away from the river toward the Latin Quarter, was there any evidence of public hostility. Here and there their progress was even marked by bursts of clapping from balconies. So far all was peaceful. But at 3 P.M. the procession, advancing peacefully on the Sorbonne, was surprised by a fierce police charge which sent it reeling back to the Boulevard St.-Germain, leaving wounded students lying in the street.

This was the opening engagement in twelve hours of violent and almost continuous skirmishing, the worst rioting Paris had known since the Algerian disorders. It was like a sudden release of aggression after long years of conscientious homework and clean collars on Sundays. the ladies who punch tickets in the metro are the descendants of those who knitted at the guillotine. The insurrec-Girls displayed as much reckless courage as boys. Masking their faces with handkerchiefs to protect themselves against the clouds of tear gas, demonstrators set fire to cars; formed human chains to throw up cobblestone barricades; attacked fire engines with sticks and stones, braving the jets; spat and screamed and fought under the savage truncheons of the police. There was an inexplicable element of demented hate in the way 10,000 young people, mostly of good family, pitted themselves against some of the best-trained and most ferocious riot police in Europe.

The all-pervasive sweet and acrid tear gas filled cafés and houses and filtered down into the metro, where, that night, hundreds of passengers rumbling back and forth under the Latin Quarter, wept in their trains, first without knowing why and then, sniffing the gas, grinning and giggling in sympathy with the students. It is no accident that

tional spirit of Paris is here provided with a highly appropriate home.

Three hundred Red Cross volunteers, linked by radio to their headquarters, braved the flying cobblestones to carry 150 wounded off the battlefield. More than 450 others, both students and police, were given first aid on the spot. The night ended with no fewer than 422 arrests.

A pattern of violence had been laid down. Great numbers of young people had learned—in the most practical of schools—the daring techniques of street fighting. Loathing for the police—and for the government which had sent them out—became unquestioned. To the observer, one of the puzzles of the May Revolution is that from the first day of serious fighting it was hard to establish at whose door responsibility should be laid. Was it the heavy hand of the police which had lit the fuse, or was it perhaps the deliberate courting of repression by small groups of hardheaded revolutionary tacticians?

"CRS-SS"—this particularly insulting slogan was scrawled on walls and chanted by demonstrators throughout the month of May. It was both unfair and inaccurate: unfair because whatever the charges against the French police, they have nothing in common with Hitler's; inaccurate because not all French police are CRS (*Compagnie Républicaine de Sécurité*), as some students supposed. There are also a uniformed city police force, lots of plainclothesmen, and a national *gendarmerie*. All these instruments went into action against the student rebels, and not all emerged with nerve and honor intact. There is a great weight of evidence—admittedly largely from student sources—to show that on regrettably numerous occasions the "forces of order" lost their heads and were inexcusably brutal, not only in the heat of battle, but to prisoners in their custody, notably in one of the detention centers of Beaujon, where large numbers of young people were held, often in extreme discomfort. One early eye-witness account in Paris was that of a Dr. Le Guen.* From his window, he saw a score of policemen attack a peaceful and crowded café, knocking people about, using their truncheons freely on faces and shins, and carting off a dozen young men to a police van. One of them, a colored boy, got into the police van under his own steam, but a quarter of an hour later an ambulance roared up to take him away on a stretcher. There was blood all over his face.

One way or another, May was a trying time for the police. They were ordered by their political masters to quell "with the utmost vigor" a series of large-scale riots, only to find the government a moment later parleying with the rioters. This seemed to leave them out on a limb, in the chill of public hostility. Not unnaturally they grew restive. Dissatisfied rumblings in the force found expression in statements by the various police unions, pinning responsibility for what they had done squarely on the government. From mid-May onward there were rumors that the police could not wholly be relied on for further repression. No doubt to restore their morale, General de Gaulle himself paid them public tribute.

Order in Paris is normally maintained by the *agents de la paix*, used mainly for directing traffic and the like, but who can—and do—turn out for riot duty, dressed in long black raincoats and carrying square shields and wooden truncheons. If they cannot cope, highly trained antiriot "intervention companies" are called in; in street combat they wear khaki denims. Both these forces are part of France's 60,000 city and municipal police, controlled in Paris by the prefecture. If further reinforcements are required, the CRS, run by the Minister of the Interior, can be asked to intervene. They are a nationwide force, 14,000 strong, deployed in the ten military districts of the country and used for fighting forest fires and mountain rescues,

* In a letter to *Le Monde* (May 9, 1968).

as well as traffic control between cities. In riots they carry round shields and long black rubber truncheons. Finally, in real emergencies, the authorities can throw into battle the 16,000-strong mobile *gendarmerie* controlled by the army and recognizable by its black jackets, blue trousers with a black stripe, and rifles. To the students they all are *flics*.

Baron Haussmann drove wide, straight boulevards through the populous labyrinth of nineteenth-century Paris to provide the emperor's troops with clear fields of fire in case of insurrection. The result was so to unite the city that now a boulevard is the natural center for insurrection, as the events of May demonstrated. "Hard luck, Baron H.: game, set, and match to the rabble."*

The main weapon on the rabble side was the *pavé*—the French cubic cobblestone, weighing about three pounds, easily prized from the roadway by determined men. On some battlefields, the demonstrators used pneumatic drills to loosen them. Barricades of *pavés,* as high as a man, were thrown up with incredible speed, providing almost unlimited supplies of ammunition. Some of the worst police casualties were caused by *pavés* received in the full face or chest, sometimes thrown from balconies with punishing effect.

The police riposte was almost as traditional: the truncheon; the gas grenade; and on rare occasions high-pressure water jets, which can knock a man down or even toss him several yards. The police were able to keep their enemy at bay, thanks to their snub-nosed grenade-throwing guns fired from the hip, with a range of more than 150 yards. Two sorts of gas grenade were used: the older CN (chloroacetophenone), which produces violent eye and throat irritation, weeping, and choking, but is made immediately harmless by water, and the more recent CS† (Ochloro-

* For a new view of Paris, see *Nairn's Paris* by Ian Nairn (London, Penguin Books, 1968).
† Known in France as CB.

benzalmalononitrile), first developed in Britain, which has three main advantages over the CN—it provokes nausea, it hangs in the air longer, and its effects are more, rather than less, disagreeable in damp conditions. CS gas in contact with water can cause nasty skin burns, as many demonstrators found to their cost, when trying to protect their faces with wet handkerchiefs. The police also threw offensive grenades, used extensively for riot control during the Algerian War and which have a blast effect. They make an intimidating noise, as thousands of Parisians who lost several nights' sleep can testify.

Professor Francis Kahn, of the Lariboisière Hospital, Paris, who prepared a report for the Russell Tribunal on the use of chemical and biological weapons in Vietnam, pronounced CS gas toxic, on evidence drawn from Vietnam and from laboratory experiments on animals. But it is perhaps significant that he did not publicly renew his charges against CS gas since his Paris press conference on May 13. The case against CS gas was not proved, and the weight of evidence from the severe fighting in Paris did not add up to a conclusive indictment. Even bitter critics of French police brutality were forced to concede that, when used under "normal circumstances"—that is, in the open air against able-bodied demonstrators—the gas caused no permanent injury. The trouble was that grenades were sometimes tossed into police vans, already crowded with demonstrators under arrest, or lobbed through windows into people's houses.

In the week beginning Monday, May 6, the current was running all the way for the students. Pompidou was still talking to the shah; De Gaulle was silent; and Peyrefitte, the young untried Minister of Education, bungled, throwing away a political career which until that moment had seemed highly promising. It was the week in which Jacques Sauvageot and Alain Geismar, the spokesmen for the students' and teachers' unions, emerged into national prominence, outdistancing in the public eye the real political leaders of the revolution and rivaling in glamor even Cohn-Bendit. It was a colossal test for these young men. It is not given to many people to lead vast, turbulent demonstrations through Paris, to take at each crossroads strategic decisions of the first importance, to conduct running negotiations with the police, to decide when to stand and fight, when to give way, when to ignore parleys and let the sheer mass of the human wave behind them carry the day. In that week the movement was at its most respectable; it aroused sympathy, not fear. The student demands at this stage carried no hint of Utopia, nothing disruptive of the social order, nothing which did not seem justified by the unhappy events of the previous few days.

They said they were ready to negotiate with M. Peyrefitte if three requests were first granted them: the withdrawal of the police from the Latin Quarter; the immediate freeing and pardoning of students either sentenced or under arrest; the reopening of the university. Everywhere they found support. Schoolboys in a score of Paris *lycées* struck in sympathy, staged sit-ins, organized strike pickets, and joined demonstrations. The *grandes écoles* themselves, the envied peaks of French elitist technocratic education, abandoned work to join the movement. Liberal professors from Nanterre and the Sorbonne went down into the street to express solidarity with the students. One of the most eloquent appeals for comprehension came from Professor Alain Touraine, the Nanterre sociologist, who had predicted the student explosion and now sought to steer it into constructive channels. He warned again that there could be no escape from a head-on clash unless repression ceased and the existence of the student movement was accepted.*

It was this ground swell which carried 30,000 students on an extraordinary five-hour romp around Paris on Tuesday, May 7, and at least that number again in a dozen

* *Le Monde* (May 11, 1968).

provincial towns. The police in serried ranks surrounded the Sorbonne, closing all approach roads. And so, since their Latin Quarter was in enemy hands, the students went elsewhere, looping round the handsome boulevards in an extravagant, joyful fifteen-mile ramble. It seemed that night as if Paris was theirs. Chanting, *"Nous sommes un groupuscule,"* they assembled in their thousands under their red and black flags, charged the thinly guarded Concorde bridge, hurled defiance at the staid, reproving *Figaro,* and swarmed up the Champs-Élysées to the Arc de Triomphe, where with fists raised, they sang the "Internationale" on the Tomb of the Unknown Soldier. Somehow their leaders brought these untidy thousands home to the Latin Quarter across the river without a single clash with the police. It was only there, after midnight, that finding the police still occupying "their" home ground, excitement and a sense of triumph broke out in a series of wild skirmishes, producing the now routine crop of destroyed cars, injured, and arrests. But on the whole it had been the students' day, a demonstration of discipline, power, and reasonableness.

This was the high point of public support for the student revolt. On May 8 the French public opinion poll IFOP reported that four-fifths of Parisians were in favor of the students. At this early stage the great mass of the bourgeoisie seemed won over. The middle classes—the parents of the demonstrators—were more incensed at police repression than concerned at the assault the students were mounting on the bourgeois state. More predictably a group of leading left-wing intellectuals, including Jean-Paul Sartre and Simone de Beauvoir, formed a Committee of Support for Student Victims of Repression. Five French Nobel Prizewinners—François Jacob, Alfred Kastler, André Lwoff, François Mauriac, and Jacques Monod—sent General de Gaulle a telegram pleading for amnesty for the students and the reopening of the university. But the general was silent.

Never in those crucial days, before the student revolt

spread to the workers, did the government by word or gesture suggest that it had grasped what the explosion was
about. Sixty thousand students throughout France had demonstrated on Tuesday, and yet at Wednesday's Cabinet
meeting Peyrefitte dismissed the crisis as the work of "spe-
cialists in agitation and elements foreign to the university."
He did no better at the emergency debate in the National
Assembly that afternoon—the first time in the history of the
Fifth Republic that the chamber, largely bypassed by De
Gaulle's style of government, had been called on to pronounce on an issue of such burning topicality. The minister
could only see the handful of *enragés*—anarchists, Castroists, and nihilists—who were at the bottom of the trouble.
He did not recognize that the movement had mushroomed
beyond them. His obtuseness must be counted as a con-
tributory factor to the savage fighting which lay ahead. "If
order is restored," he said, "all is possible; if it is not, nothing is possible." These were not sentiments to appease the
students. Gaullists, as well as opposition spokesmen, took
the minister to task, but although showing great strain, he
gave no ground. "Youth is not always right," the Socialist
leader M. Mitterrand declared. "But a society which mocks
at youth, misunderstands it, and strikes at it is always
wrong." The most moving expression of concern, mirroring
many an adult's disarray, came from a former Gaullist
minister, Edgard Pisani: "When faced by my son and his
friends, I sometimes have to keep silent or even to lie, because I am at a loss to answer their questions. . . ." Even
the Communists, who had watched the growth of the extremist movement on their left with dismay and indignation,
denouncing the *enragés* as "leftist adventurists," now re-
luctantly rallied to their support, joining their voice to the
clamor for an amnesty. But for General de Gaulle a return
to order was the first priority.

   All was now set for the clash on the terrible night of May

10-11, which echoed around the world and cracked wide
open the complacent façade of Gaullism. Confronted with a
deeply frustrated, deeply provoked student body, barely
contained by its own leaders, the government stumbled
from brutal reaction to incomprehensible inaction. It must
be held largely responsible for the subsequent disorders,
whatever part extremists played in courting a showdown.
Thursday, May 9, was probably the last occasion when
an intelligent and imaginative gesture by M. Peyrefitte
might have drawn the fuse. On Wednesday night 20,000
students had marched in peace from one boulevard to another in the Latin Quarter, guilty of nothing worse than a
few catcalls directed at the massed police standing guard at
the approaches to the Sorbonne. There was no bloodlet-
ting. The student leaders, Jacques Sauvageot and Alain
Geismar, had shown considerable courage in restraining
their more combative followers and giving the order to disperse. A word of appreciation on Thursday from Peyrefitte
might have brought a deescalation. All morning Rector
Roche and his faculty deans anxiously debated the explosive situation. At lunchtime they made public their
decision: to reopen the university and resume work.
UNEF's response was immediate: The students' strike
would go on until their three conditions had been met—
the freeing of all students under arrest; the end of court
proceedings against them; and the withdrawal of the police.
SNESup, the teachers' union, also decided to continue its
strike. That afternoon the doors of the Sorbonne remained
locked and under police guard. The minister gave no instructions to open them. He explained his firmness in a communiqué later that night: Some of the student leaders,
he said, had threatened to occupy the Sorbonne and hold
day and night meetings there, on the problems of the university; this could not be considered a return to work and
calm; the Sorbonne would remain closed. Thus, the minister torpedoed the gesture made by the rector earlier in the

day. Shortly before midnight the council of the university issued a statement expressing confidence in Rector Roche. The opportunity for appeasement had passed.

On the student front the situation now entered a more political phase. The government's intransigence gave the revolutionary hard core the opportunity to reoccupy the front of the stage and seize the initiative from the more moderate student leaders. That same Thursday night the *Jeunesse Communiste Révolutionnaire*—the Trotskyist political faction behind Cohn-Bendit—called a mass meeting at the Salle de la Mutualité, at which, for perhaps the first time since the beginning of the crisis, the extremists publicly showed their hand. So the revolt crossed the frontier from student agitation to political challenge. More than 3,000 students packed the hall in an atmosphere of feverish revolutionary ardor. Mobilized by the Trotskyists, representatives of left-wing student groups from Italy, Belgium, the Netherlands, West Germany, and Spain mounted the platform to express solidarity with their French comrades. The applause was thunderous. Cohn-Bendit was the star of the evening. "There will be no lectures so long as a single student remains in jail," he cried. Both Nanterre and the Sorbonne would be taken over by the students as soon as they were opened. So much for tactics. The strategy was laid down by Ernest Mandel, the Belgian member of the three-man unified secretariat which rules over the world Trotskyist movement. The students' struggle, he declared, "must open out into the general struggle of the working class for a Socialist revolution." Earlier that day a meeting had taken place between UNEF and France's leading trade union bosses, Georges Séguy of the CGT and Eugène Descamps of the CFDT, together representing more than 2,000,000 workers. They met to discuss the conditions for joint student-worker union action. It was a first tentative step toward Mandel's revolutionary target.

The Night of the Barricades, May 10-11, 1968, has passed into history, one of those tragic and glorious episodes that go to make up France's rich revolutionary tradition. It was a political event of first-class importance in the life of a generation—that born after, say, 1940. Seen from a distance, it may seem only one more disturbance in a disorderly month, an accidental break in the smooth graph of Gaullist rule. But for the thousands who were there that night, who felt the fear and the joy and the delirious solidarity, it will go on reverberating with the emotional power of a first love affair. As with all truly revolutionary moments, its ultimate consequences may not be visible for years.

It all began with the teen-agers, at least 5,000 of them, their blood up. *Libérez nos camarades!* This was the cry, as they marched, red and black flags flying, into the Place Denfert-Rochereau, a vast untidy crossroads, near Montparnasse, with the old stone "Lion de Belfort" at its center. From the "Lion," high above the crowd, the schoolboy leaders of the *Comités d'Action Lycéens* (CAL's) worked them up with all the skill and the oratory of seasoned politicians. They were waiting at the rendezvous set by UNEF and SNESup for the great demonstration planned as the students' and teachers' riposte to the government's refusal to give way. And they were early. Since December, 1967 —in a bare five months—the CAL's had grown (especially in Paris) into a formidable left-wing pressure group, largely under JCR inspiration. They represented the rapid spread of radical ideas to a whole generation of preuniversity age, stamping the May Revolution with a gay, teenage freshness. As they waited in the sunshine at Denfert-Rochereau, their leaders sang out the great themes of schoolboy militancy: freedom for political action in the *lycée;* recognition by the school authorities of the CAL's; a share for the pupils in the running of their schools. These boys and girls were the demolition crews preparing to dynamite the old barracks of French secondary education.

At last the older brothers and sisters appeared and the teen-agers were soon merged in a great crowd, perhaps 15,000 strong. It was at that moment, about 6:30 P.M., that word reached the student leaders of new conciliatory proposals from Louis Joxe, the Acting Premier. He offered the immediate withdrawal of police from the Latin Quarter, permission for the students to hold a meeting there that night, and the reopening of the Sorbonne on Saturday. These proposals were put to the crowd. Their answer was a great roar of *Libérez nos camarades!* The government's gesture had come too late. Student opinion had hardened. And so the vast gathering moved off toward the nearby Santé Prison, where the students thought their comrades were being held. Massed police kept them away from the prison walls, but hands reached out from barred windows to wave to them. Arms linked and wearing an assortment of crash helmets, a front rank of hard-core militants strained to contain the crowd and steer it toward the Maison de la Radio, the great circular temple of the French state broadcasting system on the Right Bank of the Seine.

But motorcycle couriers brought news that all the bridges across the river were blocked by police vans parked bumper to bumper. The demonstration, deprived of its target, swept down the Boulevard St.-Germain on the Left Bank; here again its progress was barred by strong forces of police forcing it ineluctably up the Boulevard St.-Michel toward the Sorbonne. It was as if the authorities had chosen to risk battle on the students' own ground in the Latin Quarter. The leaders met for hurried consultations. After a week of mounting frustration, they could not propose leading their restive troops back to Denfert-Rochereau; they would not have been followed. Like a flash, the order went out: "The *quartier* must be ours at whatever cost!" Immediately, as if obeying some profound mob instinct, the demonstrators fanned out through the familiar labyrinth of student Paris, like guerrillas on their home terrain. On every alleyway and approach road leading to the university, the police found themselves confronted with rebel troops, who, like busy termites, started tearing up gratings and traffic signs and burrowing down through the Tarmac to the *pavés*. No order was sent out, but perhaps at first from a feeling of exposure, perhaps because, as they waited, the students had nothing better to do, barricades sprang up. On such a dispersed front, there can be no certainty about what exactly happened, but the first barricade—a makeshift thing of overturned cars and assorted debris—was seen at about 9:15 in the Rue le Goff, a stone's throw from the southern wall of the Sorbonne. Before the night was out, there were at least sixty, some of them formidable constructions of piled *pavés,* so swiftly and yet neatly built that the belief has spread that young workers came to the aid of the students. Thus has that night entered revolutionary legend: The barricades, an ancient symbol of insurrection here revived, brought about the marriage of intellectuals and workers of which revolutionaries dream.

As news reached the students that the police had called up heavy reinforcements, the throwing up of barricades became more feverish. Building sites were plundered, billboards torn down from the walls, scaffolding and barbed wire piled up, and everywhere cars were tipped on their sides and jammed in among the *pavés.* Anxiety was blotted out by a sort of frenetic joy. They were like men preparing to sell their lives dearly.

Shortly after 10 P.M., Rector Roche, in a desperate bid to head off a clash, broadcast an appeal from the Sorbonne to the student leaders, inviting them to meet him there and then. An extraordinary exchange followed, between Vice-Rector Chalin and Alain Geismar, the SNESup spokesman, conducted as publicly as any negotiation in history—over the radio. Radio Luxembourg reporters in mobile radio vans had got hold of the two men and put them on the air. Geismar declared there could be no talks until the arrested students were released and amnestied. The students thus posed a condition which it was not in the power of the university authorities to concede. The impasse seemed total. But hope of a settlement welled up again shortly after midnight when it was learned that Cohn-Bendit, together with a group of teachers and students, were after all locked in session with Rector Roche, who, in turn, had been on the telephone to M. Peyrefitte, the Education Minister. These hopes were soon dashed. Cohn-Bendit emerged with the words: "We told the rector that what is happening in the street tonight is a whole generation rising against a certain sort of society. We told him blood would flow if the police did not leave the Latin Quarter. We know the demonstrators will stay behind the barricades until our three demands have been met." At 1:15 it was clear there could be no peaceful way out. The vice-rector declared: "We have tried to negotiate. We have tried by all possible means to avoid the use of force, but the situation is now out of our control. We have failed." An hour later the first wave of police stormed the first student defenses.

The decision to attack was taken by a small group of ministers and senior Élysée officials who met in virtually permanent session all night. At the center of these somber and anxious talks was the Acting Premier, Louis Joxe, advised by Christian Fouchet (Interior), Pierre Messmer (Army), Georges Gorse (Information), and the luckless Alain Peyrefitte. From the Élysée came Bernard Tricot, De Gaulle's right-hand man, and Jacques Foccart, believed to be the President's adviser on security and intelligence. The inescapable conclusion is that the government's security advisers overrode the repeated appeals for leniency made by Rector Roche. (The next day the university council expressed its unanimous regret that Roche's advice had not been taken.)

After the savagery of that night's fighting, there was no going back for the student revolutionaries. The movement had acquired its own terrible dynamic. Drawn by the battle commentaries on the independent radio networks, thousands of young people, many of them workers, raced across Paris to join in. It was a free-for-all on a scale to satisfy every repressed dream. The riot police first volleyed in their gas grenades to stampede the enemy troops and then charged into the breach to capture the barricades. There was stiff hand-to-hand fighting in the choking air. The wounded fell and could not be rescued. Then, to slow the grinding advance of the CRS, the defenders set fire to their barrages. The thud of exploding gasoline tanks could be heard across the river on the Right Bank. Ernest Mandel, the Trotskyist Fourth International leader from Brussels, climbed onto a barricade, gazed at the spectacle of fire and desolation and exclaimed joyfully, in his heavy Belgian accent: *"Ah! Comme c'est beau! C'est la révolution!"* He was watching his own car burning.

The Trotskyist youth group, the JCR, played a prominent part in the struggle. Their mass meeting the previous night, to which Cohn-Bendit and several other student leaders had come, confirmed their position as the leading political faction behind the revolt. Their *service d'ordre* (under the command of Yves Niaudet and an Egyptian Copt, Jean Labib) had guarded the front and the flanks of the demonstration. Now their leaders, Alain Krivine and Henri Weber, ordered the hard-core militants to split up into small groups and help man the barricades. This front-line role stood the JCR in good stead. Their ultra-sectarian rivals, the FER, fared less well. Some 300 to 400 of their shock troops arrived on the battlefield shortly after midnight in almost military formation, but at the sight of the barricades, their leader were seized by doctrinal doubts: This was clearly going to be murder. It was an "adventurist" enterprise, in which the FER would have no part. Their squad marched off the field to the derisive hoots of the embattled students.

FER's defection at the hour of combat will long be remembered.

A small German SDS contingent fought by the side of their French comrades (and French police were seen assiduously taking down the German registration numbers of Volkswagens parked that night in the Latin Quarter), but they were not as numerous as they would have wished. That week two SDS leaders, Rabehl and Semmler, were turned back at Orly Airport, and a busload of German student actors was stopped at the Strasbourg frontier post when border police found in their coach helmets, truncheons, and revolutionary tracts, as well as Chinese and Vietcong flags.

Lit by the red glare from the fires and under drifting acrid gas clouds, the battle raged for four hours, as the police in charge after charge drove the students from their defenses, pinning them into an ever smaller redoubt from which they could escape only by braving the fury of rifle butts and truncheons. Residents of the *quartier,* horrified spectators of the savage mopping-up operations, passed food and drink to the insurgents, doused them in water to allay the tear gas, and took fleeing and bleeding students into their houses, from which only too often they were snatched by the police. One girl, who had not taken part in the demonstrations, was attacked in her room by police, stripped, and driven into the street naked.*

Red Cross volunteers were themselves sometimes felled by truncheons, and their patients dragged from stretchers for further beating.

Boys and girls threw themselves into the fighting with incredible abandon and dedication. To many young and high-keyed spirits, this was the chance to join the heroic revolution of Frantz Fanon, Che Guevara, and Régis Debray, to which they had so long thrilled. This was their Vietnam. There was about the events that night an ele-

* Letter to *Le Monde* from Daniel Moureaud (May 15, 1968).

ment of the cinema, not only in the dramatic settings, but
in the great self-consciousness of the young actors. In
deadly earnest, they were playing a game of guerrillas,
acting out the colonial revolution in the heart of a Western capital. In this war game the sinister and terrifying
police—masked, goggled, helmeted, clad in gleaming black
from head to toe—were cast in the role of evil spirits,
initiating the innocent to the cruelty and bestiality of the
world. It is at such highly charged moments that politics
bite into the mind. *"De Gaulle assassin!"* a thousand young
throats cried.

At 4:20 in the morning the ministers gathered at the
Interior Ministry issued a brief defensive communiqué.
At 5:30 Cohn-Bendit gave the order for dispersal over
the radio. At 6, exhausted and unshaved, Louis Joxe,
Christian Fouchet, Pierre Messmer, and Jacques Foccart
drove to the Élysée to report to President de Gaulle that
the insurrection had been crushed. The balance sheet: 367
wounded; 460 taken into custody; 188 cars damaged or
destroyed; incalculable quantities of hate.

On Friday, May 10, 1968, Americans and North Vietnamese made their first contacts in Paris, the world's
"peace capital."

Herbert Marcuse, the German-American philosopher
often credited with paternity for the world student revolt,
was also in Paris that weekend, taking part in a UNESCO
conference on Marx. He spoke of the new catalysts for
revolution in industrial countries, men living on the fringes
of society such as the outcasts of black ghettos—and the
students.

On Saturday night, May 11, Georges Pompidou, Prime
Minister of France, returned to Paris from Afghanistan.
Burnt-out cars still littered the Latin Quarter after the
Night of the Barricades. Barely three hours after his ar-
rival, M. Pompidou addressed the nation. Three minutes

later he, singled-handed, had reversed the whole current of government policy. Toughness, obstinacy, repression gave way to sweet understanding. The Sorbonne, he announced, would be freely open from Monday, and the Court of Appeal would pronounce on the jailed students. The clear implications were that the police would be withdrawn and the students released. From any other man, this climb-down would have been a defeat. Pompidou turned it into a personal victory. Luckily for him, he had been out of the country when the disturbances took place and, therefore, could not be held responsible for the violent turn they took. Moreover, his conciliatory decisions marked him as the one man in the government who could influence General de Gaulle. *"Pompidou a dit 'je,' "* *L' Express,* the French weekly, reported, in a sly reference to the Prime Minister's increased authority.

But he was like a man trying to stop an avalanche. At five o'clock that Saturday morning students invaded Strasbourg University, hoisted a red flag, and proclaimed the university's "autonomy" from the Ministry of Education in Paris. They stockpiled food and set up their own militia, while hundreds of schoolchildren came out in their support and distributed tracts to the people of Strasbourg to support the students against police repression. This mutiny was a direct reaction to the street fighting in Paris, which Strasbourg students had indignantly followed on their transistor radios all night. In Paris on Saturday afternoon a small force of about forty militants of the *Mouvement d'Action Universitaire* (MAU)* occupied an annex of the faculty of letters in the Rue Censier. This was a deliberate insurrectional act. They chose the Censier Annex because it was unguarded, whereas the Sorbonne itself was surrounded by thousands of police. The MAU leadership was agreed that a university building must at all costs be occupied, and a general discussion opened. The debate raged,

* See page 62.

almost without interruption, for two days and nights, from
Saturday night to Monday. It was the first impassioned explosion of talk in the capital. How could the students give
new impetus to a movement born in the streets? How could
the university be transformed so that it could in turn transform society? Thus began, in Paris and the provinces, the
wave of occupations and tireless debate which marked the
May Revolution, spreading with breakneck speed from university to factory, until industry and the public services
were paralyzed.

M. Pompidou was too late to stop the linkup between
workers and students. That Saturday morning the two
most powerful union federations, the CGT and the CFDT,
together with the FEN,* France's major teachers' federation, called on their members to strike and demonstrate on Monday, May 13, the tenth anniversary of the
Algiers putsch which had brought De Gaulle to power.
It was clear that the protest was intended as a political
challenge to the regime, a loaded birthday present for
the general.

For all his skill, M. Pompidou on his return that night
underestimated the strength of public feeling running
against the government. Giving in to the students' demands,
as he did, was not enough. The opposition dailies, *L'Humanité* and *Combat,* had rushed out special afternoon
editions to shriek their indignation at the violence of police repression. Hundreds of anxious parents whose children were missing were besieging hospitals and police
stations. The revolution had started some hours before
Pompidou landed at Orly; it would have to run its course.

The immense demonstration, some 800,000 strong, on
Monday, May 13, was a landmark. It marched from the
Gare de l'Est across the river to the Place Denfert-Rocher-
eau, a political riposte for the Night of the Barricades.
By forcing the unions to strike in their favor, by bringing

* See footnote, page 63.

such hordes into the streets, the student leaders demonstrated once and for all that they were no longer a lunatic-fringe *groupuscule,* but a national force. They managed to touch something very profound in the conscience of the country, and here, in the massed ranks of workers and in the countless fluttering banners, was the proof of it. They were proved right, and those who had sneered at them at the start were proved wrong. They seemed to speak a language which others understood; their folly suddenly seemed reasonable. "It was an extraordinary day," Alain Geismar, the SNESup leader, declared. "The students left the university ghetto to join the workers who had left the ghetto of the factory. Those who had fought in the street met up with those who had looked on. The workers now joined the struggle."* Perhaps recognizing this new force, the authorities kept the police well out of sight.

Geismar, Sauvageot, and Cohn-Bendit, marching with their arms around one another's shoulders, led the 800,000, taking triumphant precedence over the union bosses, Georges Séguy of the CGT and Eugène Descamps of the CFDT. Way back, buried in the crowd, came the left-wing politicians, François Mitterrand, Guy Mollet, Pierre Mendès-France, Waldeck Rochet. They received no deference from the student organizers; they were firmly kept away from the front of the cortege. The young revolutionaries wanted no one to muscle in on their act, no political party to take them over. As usual it was Cohn-Bendit who most pungently expressed their contempt for the official left: "The Communist Party? Nothing gave me greater pleasure than to be at the head of a demonstration with all that Stalinist filth in the rear." To the alarm of their union leaders, many young workers seemed to thrill to the students' slogans. The virus was spreading to the base of the labor force and eating away at the leaders' authority.

* J. Sauvageot, A. Geismar, D. Cohn-Bendit, and J.-P. Duteuil, *La Révolte Étudiante* (Paris, Seuil, 1968), p. 56.

This great *journée* was the occasion for the issue of new, more militant directives. "The strike will go on!" declared Jacques Sauvageot. "All university buildings will be occupied! Our aim is absolutely free political discussions inside the university, as well as the resignation of the Minister of the Interior and the Prefect of Police." Cohn-Bendit called for action committees to be set up in every firm and in every area of Paris. For those who knew where to look, the young Trotskyists of the JCR, under their leader Alain Krivine, were there in force. It was they who provided the student police force, the all-important *service d'ordre,* which gave the massive demonstration its shape; which controlled traffic along the route; and which, after the workers had dispersed on orders from their leaders, led a student contingent to an open-air meeting beneath the Eiffel Tower on the Champ de Mars, that ancient parade ground, which during the 1789 Revolution had seen many gatherings of discontented citizenry. And then the students dispersed to the cry of "Everyone to the Sorbonne!"

Pompidou had kept his promise: The imprisoned students had been released; the police had pulled back from the Latin Quarter; the gates of the Sorbonne stood open. The students surged in and took possession. That was the first night of the Student Soviet—an extraordinary example of primitive Communism in the heart of a Western industrial country—which was not to end till their expulsion thirty-four days later on June 16. Fired by the students' example, the workers too struck and occupied, first at an aircraft plant at Nantes on Tuesday and then like wildfire throughout France. How were these soviets organized, what was the mood of this novel experiment, what has remained? These are some of the questions which the following pages will seek to answer.

5   Background to Revolution

To live through a revolution is a delirious experience. It is a little frightening, but also exhilarating, to see authority flouted and then routed. In the two or three weeks after the Night of the Barricades, France was in a state of revolution. That is to say, the existing power structure—not only political power, but every sort of power—was challenged and in some cases overthrown, and an attempt was made, however confused and disorderly, to put another in its stead. Students, workers, active citizens joined together spontaneously in hundreds of insurrectional committees all over Paris, but also in the provinces. This very widespread revolt against the old forms of established authority was accompanied by an acute and profoundly enjoyable sense of liberation. All sorts of people felt it in all walks of life. A great gust of fresh air blew through dusty minds and offices and bureaucratic structures. This throwing off of constraint, this sense of relief was the authentic stamp of the revolution, the proof that the changes being wrought were really of revolutionary proportions.

Suddenly and for a few precious days, the French, whose normal life is bound by many petty regulations, enjoyed the pleasures of a primitive anarchistic society. It was a society without policemen, with everyone his own traffic cop. In spite of the vexations of life, the strike, and the drying up of gasoline pumps, men will look back on that period and remember it with joy.

The most striking feature of those days was the sight

of people talking to one another—not only casual exchanges, but long intense conversations between total strangers, clustered at street corners, in cafés, in the Sorbonne, of course. There was an explosion of talk, as if people had been saving up what they had to say for years. And what was impressive was the tolerance with which they listened to one another, as if all those endless dialogues were a form of group therapy. Many French men and women woke up to the fact that their relations with one another had been far too stiff and suspicious, far too unfraternal. It seemed as if the system were wrong: children not speaking freely to their parents; employees touching their caps to the bosses; the whole nation standing to attention before the general and his vision of France.

General de Gaulle's decade of rule is doubtless among the major causes of the May outburst. His paternalism, the control he has exerted over information, the cant and pomp of his style of government, irritate and do not impress the young. They run counter to the irreverent, skeptical, iconoclastic spirit of the age. But De Gaulle is not alone to blame. The explosion was a reaction to the way power has been exercised in France, not only since De Gaulle but since Napoleon—and at every level.

More than most countries, and certainly more than Britain, the United States, or West Germany, France is burdened with a centralized, profoundly hierarchical government bureaucracy. All decisions, even footling ones, are made in Paris. The provinces fret and fume and send memoranda to the distant ministry. Everywhere the petty bureaucrat sits, passing up the dossier to his hierarchical superior, jealously exercising his own limited authority according to the rulebook. "Napoleon is at last dead, and the longest reign in French history is over," a commentator in *Le Monde,* Gilbert Cesbron, wrote after the events of May.*

* *Le Monde* (June 26, 1968).

But the rigidities of government service are also characteristic of French professional life. At the top of most
professional trees sits a mandarin—or a *grand patron* as
the French sometimes say—behaving like a prince, delegating neither authority nor rights. This may be something
of a caricature, but it was on the whole true that before
the great shake-up of May the channels of advancement
in very many walks of life were blocked by red tape, out-
worn tradition, and men who were there for life. It was
against all these mandarinates in universities, factories, trade
unions, and professions that the revolution released a flood
of impatience and defiance. No authority was spared.
Wherever in the routine of daily life orders were given and
were expected to be obeyed, someone got up to challenge
the system.

To revolt, then, was directed against the way French
society is organized. To this extent it was a specifically
French phenomenon. But it may also turn out to be the
first outburst against the streamlined tyranny of an advanced Western state. If this is true, it has a more general significance. In the last fifteen-odd years, France has
attempted to get into big-time international competition.
The scramble to modernize, after centuries of protection-
ism, disturbed patterns of life, as did the consumer goods
which began to flood the French market. All the workers
wanted more of them, a bigger share of the cake, but
some hated the harsh boring discipline of the assembly
line and regretted the old craftsman's independence; others
found jarring and distasteful the brisk, highly competitive
chromium-plated world sold by advertising jingles. Labor
relations in French industry tend to be primitive by British
or American standards. Skilled workers, clerks, junior
managers wanted more information about what was going
on in their works; they wanted a share in the decisions
which affected them directly; they wanted stronger and

more active union leadership. All these grievances and a
thousand others fed the explosion of May.

The most original and creative phase of the revolution
was the last three weeks of May, from the Night of the
Barricades to De Gaulle's prodigious recovery on May 30.
It was then that a new political vocabulary emerged, drawing the crowd into action as allies of the young revolutionary leaders. It was then that insurrectional committees sprang up, embodying the thirst for decentralization,
as well as the urge to run one's own affairs, which lay
at the root of the revolt. From the start of their protest
movement, the revolutionaries preached direct action as
opposed to negotiation. Now the slogan was Direct Democracy as opposed to the classic delegation of powers within a parliamentary system. Both in direct action and in
direct democracy was present the notion of permanent
contestation—the view that the bourgeois state and all
its institutions must be subject to constant harassment and
questioning. Nothing was to be taken for granted. The
contestation could equally well take the form of mobbing
a professor, of occupying a faculty, of defying the power
of the state by a street demonstration, of locking a factory manager into his office.

Everywhere, from one end of France to another, action
committees were spontaneously formed at grass-roots level,
forums of debate, as well as of decision. They were the
translation into practical (but often impractical) terms
of the twin notions of direct action and direct democracy.
These action committees were conceived as the agents of
revolutionary change. They were to be the forerunners
of a totally new type of society, in which everyone had the
right to talk and the right to share in decision making.
These committees—at least 450 of which were set up
in those three weeks of May, with widely different func-
tions and membership—were the most characteristic expression of the revolution. They justified the claim that

new and original power structures, new revolutionary channels of authority, were emerging. The revolutionaries, in
their enthusiasm, used such terms as *structures parallèles*
and *double pouvoir*.

To many, these ideas and the forms they took seemed
deliriously novel. This was not so. There were echoes in
the May Revolution of Russia, of the 1918 revolution
in Germany, of Spain, and of Cuba (indeed, some naïve
but ardent spirits are said to have put through long-distance
telephone calls to Moscow and Havana to seek advice on
how to proceed). Above all, the revolutionaries were inspired by the history of France, by the mood and architecture of Paris, by the memories of violent upheaval just
below the surface of French consciousness. The action
committees, for example, formed in the twenty *arrondissements* of Paris were the direct heirs of the committees
of sans-culottes which ran the forty-eight sections of Paris
in 1790. Both then and now, these were committees of
active and militant citizens. They were also the place where
systematic indoctrination in the aims and jargon of the
revolution took place. In 1789 the wineshops were another potent channel of communication for revolutionary
ideas. It was here that the *menu peuple* (common people)
gathered to gossip and exchange news. In 1968 this was
the role played by the sidewalk discussions and by the
cafés on the boulevards of the Latin Quarter, each a nest
of insurgents. Many paid the price. Le Luxembourg, for
instance, a popular café on the Boulevard St.-Michel, was
stormed by police one wild night. At closing time the
manager threw out his hands and said with magnificent
aplomb: "Gentlemen, tonight Le Luxembourg will not
close its doors; it has none left!"

In 1789 pamphleteers and revolutionary journalists used
to congregate nightly to acquire the slogans which gave
a positive course to the movement. Similarily this year
the revolutionary leaders met each night to issue direc-

tives for the pamphlets, tracts, street posters, and revolutionary journals which played a big part in shaping popular opinion. Men like Cohn-Bendit, Jacques Sauvageot, and Alain Geismar were undoubtedly an important element in mobilizing the demonstrations, but the crowds that surged through Paris and manned the barricades were far from being passive instruments; their political awareness was of a very high level. Almost any one of them, if asked, could have explained what the revolt was about in the "right" jargon. They had absorbed and adapted the slogans and ideas of the avant-garde political groups that triggered the disturbances. In this they resembled the revolutionary crowds of 1789, fired by the new ideas of liberty and the rights of man, who with more or less articulateness knew that what they were after was a change in the forms of executive power. Again, as in 1789, a piece of news, even sometimes only a rumor, could transform a good-humored, relatively harmless demonstration into a riot of insurrectionary proportions. For example, in the summer of 1789, a peacefully disposed Sunday crowd of strollers in the Palais Royal was galvanized into revolutionary vigor by the news of Necker's dismissal.* In the same way, in Paris last June, a report that a schoolboy had drowned in the Seine when fleeing from a police charge sparked off a citywide cycle of violence. What could be more like the *journées révolutionnaires* of the first French Revolution—days of revolutionary struggle in which mobs of sans-culottes took part—than the three bloody Fridays of May, 1968? Much of the vocabulary seemed almost consciously borrowed from the past. Cohn-Bendit and his friends called themselves the *enragés* in tribute to the group of extremists, led by Jacques Roux, Théophile Leclerc, and Jean Varlet, who so influenced the sans-culottes in 1793. Almost every Paris newspaper last May

* See George Rudé, *The Crowd in the French Revolution* (London, Oxford University Press), 1959, p. 220.

described the Sorbonne as the headquarters of the student Commune, the title given to the Paris local government that emerged after the fall of the Bastille. And how often did the Ministry of the Interior denounce the handful of *meneurs,* troublemaking leaders straight out of revolutionary history?

6 Experiments in Revolution: The Student Soviet

> The government has lost control of its faculties.
> *Le Canard Enchaîné*

FOR just over a month, from May 13 to June 16, 1968, the Sorbonne was the central fortress of the Student Soviet. When it fell, the heart was knocked out of this Utopia. While it held, it inspired the whole Latin Quarter to exultant insurrection, to become a free state within the Gaullist empire. The Sorbonne under student management is perhaps the most eloquent symbol of the May Revolution. It was both a political laboratory, in which the students tested out their theories of direct democracy, and an example which fired the workers, if not to do likewise, at least to strike and occupy their factories.

It is hard to write coherently of the Sorbonne in those fantastic days because it was itself so incoherent, so disorderly, such an explosion of contradictions. The building is a vast rectangle, more than 250 yards long, lying just off the Boulevard St.-Michel, but totally different in character from the striped awnings and extravagant informality of the sidewalk cafés. To penetrate through the narrow archway of the Sorbonne is to enter a world of heavy-handed, rather utilitarian classicism, where Victor Hugo and Louis Pasteur sit brooding in stone over the courtyard. Corridors march off into the body of the building, and staircases wind upward to a labyrinth of offices and lecture rooms. The solemn core of the building is the *Grand Amphithéâtre,* dominated by an immense, infinitely wooden, mural by Puvis de Chavannes, depicting poetry, philosophy, geometry, and other assorted branches of knowledge surrounding a seated figure representing the Sorbonne. This was the unpromising setting for the joyful and irreverent torrent which swept through the French university in May.

It is a building in which 6,000 people could elegantly be housed. Imagine 20,000—perhaps indeed 30,000—filling the flagged courtyard to bursting point, fighting their way along jammed passages, climbing over one another's shoulders for the nonstop debates in the groaning amphitheaters, where confused, wordy, violent opinions are hurled into the microphones. Everywhere, on every story, is a hurrying, scurrying stream, some obviously functionaries carrying dossiers, others in the red armbands of the *service d'ordre*. Every room is occupied. What exactly is happening? What in this ant heap is central to the Student Soviet and what peripheral? The truth is that the occupied Sorbonne was a mirror of the student movement, lucid and yet crazy, calculated and yet spontaneous. A revolutionary avant-garde knew more or less what was going on and provided a minimum infrastructure of ideas and organization, around which flourished a rank garden of weeds and flowers, fertile and unplanned.

Within hours of its occupation the walls of the Sorbonne were covered with wild, joyful graffiti, and the formal classical courtyard, festooned with red and black flags and decorated with portraits of Mao, Lenin and Marx, Trotsky, Castro and Guevara, became a bazaar for trafficking in revolutionary ideas. A youngster thumped out jazz tunes at a grand piano. Scores of young people just lay about in this august place hugging one another, plucking guitars, thronging the chapel steps, thumbing their noses at the grown-up world which would have them stand up straight and comb their hair. They had played the guerrilla game; now they just played, rediscovering with shameless self-consciousness the fun and eroticism to be had from life. "The more I make revolution, the more I feel like making love," they scrawled on the wall. All this theatrical side of the young people's revolt was a genuine, even an essential part of the experiment. From some adults it drew raised eyebrows or envious reproof; others recognized it as the instinctual counterpart to the hardheaded planning which was also taking place. The extravaganza was welcome to the revolutionary leaders and yet also a nuisance, because difficult to control and ultimately discreditable. Was not "It is forbidden to forbid" one of the key slogans on the Sorbonne walls? Half a dozen leaders met daily to decide what to do next, what slogans and directives to issue, what structure to give their Tower of Babel. They wanted the Sorbonne and its store of knowledge to be free and open to all; they wanted everyone to have a right to speak; they wanted each student to feel responsible for his own intellectual attitudes. This, after all, was the point of rejecting the cramping, outdated spoon-feeding of the past.

Gradually, through trial and error, out of feverish debate, took shape a tentative command structure. Simply to describe it is to ignore the countless changes, accretions, squabbles of that hectic month. At the base, and in theory the source of all sovereignty, was the general assembly, a vast, shapeless mob which nightly packed the *Grand Amphithéâtre*. This was direct democracy in action, a talking shop of infinite permissiveness. One of the first acts of the first General Assembly on May 13 was to declare the Sorbonne an autonomous popular university, open day and night to all workers. In principle all decisions taken in the building had to be put to the assembly for approval. Each night the assembly elected a fifteen-man Occupation Committee, which was the seat of executive power. Its mandate was limited to a single day and night on the theory that power corrupts and that every elected representative must constantly give an account of himself to his electors. The bureaucracy must not be given time to ossify. (The system did not, alas, last beyond the first few days. Soon the whole of Paris came to goggle at the Sorbonne—many a smart dinner party ended the evening there rubbing shoulders with the ravishing teen-agers—and the assemblies degenerated into disorderly "happenings," leaving the Occupation Committee more or less unchallenged.)

The Occupation Committee bred or inspired a score of subcommittees to handle catering, press relations, the dormitory, the *service d'ordre,* the infirmary, the "bank," to which funds collected in the courtyard or around the cafés were channeled. Paper had to be bought for the tracts, and ink, and food for the night workers. Someone had to be given a hundred francs to buy dressings for a wounded militant hidden across town in a friend's apartment. Another key committee kept a tally of rooms and allocated them to spontaneously formed groups that wanted somewhere to debate and conduct their business. One could see an eager gaggle of boys and girls bursting into an empty office, posting up on the door who they were and what they were about, and then sending a courier off to the Rooms Committee to lay formal claim to their premises. They would appoint a chairman and secretary, hold their debate, draft a motion, and then fight their way downstairs to the *Grand Amphi* to present it to the masses. There were committees organized on a department basis, in which teachers joined the students—historians in one room, geographers in another, a group of *anglicistes* in a third. But there were also rooms in which Africans debated Third World problems in impeccable French, rooms in which the challenging problems of sexual repression were explored, and yet others in which, later in the evening, such problems were surmounted. A Commission of Cultural Agitation sat in more or less permanent session, staging alternating performances and discussions. Here a motion to plaster over Puvis de Chavannes' fresco, "Ancient Greece Unveiling Herself Before Archeology," was narrowly defeated. Anxious teenagers with furrowed brows tirelessly debated the place of art in a capitalistic society, or the destructive powers of a gadget civilization, or simply the eternal imponderables of the human couple. A *comité de témoignages,* run with adult help, took down verbatim accounts of instances of police brutality, which were later published by Seuil as a black book, a horrifying indictment of a would-be civilized society. Girls, often with more staying power and fervor than boys, typed, cut stencils, cooked, looked after children in the nursery, made beds in the improvised communal dormitories. For the thousands of young people taking part, it was a delirious and unforgettable experience, one of the most formative they might ever live through. If the May Revolution was anything at all, it was this roaring mass of spontaneous student committees and assemblies running its own affairs.

One issue divided the Student Soviet from the start and was never satisfactorily resolved. This was the struggle between reformists and revolutionaries. On one side were those who saw the student revolt as a means of putting pressure on the government to reconstruct the universities in France on a wholly new basis. They dreamed of autonomous, decentralized campuses, of the overthrow of the remote mandarins, of throwing wide the universities to the working class. On the other hand were those for whom university reform was a troublesome irrelevance. The fighting at the barricades had aroused in them the hope of revolutionary action. They wanted to march, red flag flying, from the rubble of the university on society itself—and in particular on President de Gaulle's regime. In the words of Edgar Morin, one of the most perceptive commentators on the French crisis, they wanted to turn the courtyard of the Sorbonne into the launching pad of a revolutionary missile.

Stiffened by the Trotskyists, the leadership was, of course, for revolution. To outdistance and defeat the reformists, it galloped ahead, throwing its troops into action —action at all costs and by all possible means—according to the logic of permanent revolution. This often took a nasty turn. From the sanctuary of the Sorbonne, students sallied forth time and again to tear up the roadway, smash windows, and set fire to cars, within a stone's throw of the police station. They escaped arrest by fleeing to the immunity of the university courtyard. But with this increasingly pointless violence, the movement outran its strength and was cut down.

With their more modest objectives, the reformists may have secured a more permanent achievement. The French university has now to be rebuilt, virtually from scratch. In this task, the legacy of May is likely to be threefold: a new and healthier teacher-student relationship; a certain measure of local autonomy both at faculty and provincial university level; a far greater share by the students in the planning and running of their studies. In planning these reforms, the state must inevitably take into account the detailed proposals—some running to documents hundreds of pages long—which students and teachers drafted throughout the crisis.

The Sorbonne was the most spectacular of all the student occupations, but much the same tale could be told of almost every other faculty in Paris and the provinces. Everywhere there was the same explosion of talk and fun, the same poetic graffiti, the same thirst for cultural liberation, the same hostility to the regime. The movement overran such august establishments as the Collège de France and the Centre National de la Recherche Scientifique. It invaded the traditionally right-wing schools of law, medicine, and political science. Even theological students "militated" in their seminaries, as well as the overbred young men of the École Polytechnique. Everywhere spirits were unmuzzled, and intellectual dikes burst in a splendidly wasteful release of youthful energy.

As far as the general public was concerned, perhaps the most influential revolt was that of the *École Nationale des Beaux-Arts* in the Rue Bonaparte which, from the moment of its occupation on May 14, was transformed into a semi-clandestine, insurrectional poster factory. The most active young painters of the École de Paris became the iconographers of the revolution, covering the walls of Paris with cartoons of great savagery and punch. The Beaux-Arts was, like so much of French education, dull, fossilized, hierarchical. Here, too, there were *grands patrons,* stifling the studios with the weight of their prestige. May changed all that. Where once a few dozen students came to work, the occupation brought at least 1,000, who, in teams of about 200, worked day and night. The output was prodigious; at least 100,000 posters were run off with some 350 original designs. They are rapidly becoming collectors' items. Here, too, a sort of direct democracy operated. Designs were submitted to a General Assembly of students and teachers, and a vote was taken. The school was finally cleared by the police on June 27, but after the experience of May, it is hard to envisage any future reform in which the students will not play an active part.

Not all the student initiatives were as coherent or as productive. On May 15, two days after the occupation of the Sorbonne, when euphoria was at its height, a student column, some hundreds strong, marched on the Théâtre de France at the Odéon and occupied it, surging in as the audience left after a performance of the American Paul Taylor ballet. Jean-Louis Barrault, director of the theatre, bowed to the inevitable with the words: "Barrault is dead!" This invasion seemed to have important revolutionary implications: It was the first time the student revolt overspilled the frontiers of the university. It presaged further attacks on state property. There were rumors that it was merely a dress rehearsal for an assault on the Maison de la Radio, the bastion symbolizing the Gaullist regime's ruthless control of information. In a modern telecommunications society, the radio station is one of the real seats of authority, its seizure the seal of a successful revolution. In the Prime Minister's office and at the Ministry of the Interior, there was a sense of horrifying danger, a premonition of real— and probably bloody—revolution. What if the student rabble army really did set out to conquer Paris and what if the Communist-led union federation, the most powerful popular force in the country, threw its weight behind them? In the event neither threat materialized: The march on the radio station was put off and then canceled; the unions, as we shall see in Chapter Ten, doggedly refused to be stampeded. The occupation of the Odéon was a baroque unmeditated gesture, a flourish on the margin of the revolution, not part of the mainstream. It was inspired by Cohn-Bendit's March 22 Movement, according to the spontaneous strategy he advocated, without consultation with the more hardheaded groups which made up the revolutionary leadership.

In the month of its occupation the "ex-Théâtre de France" was open day and night as a sort of revolutionary forum, club, and flophouse. No plays were put on, only countless wordy, marathon debates. It was an experiment denounced by the students' union, UNEF, as well as by the French Actors' Union. As the days passed, groups of squatters came and went, plundering the wardrobes for theatrical costumes and thus confronting the police in the street skirmishes with an army of extras. A tramp made his home in this temple of direct democracy, rising from time to time to intervene in the debates from his seat in the gallery. *"Eh bien,"* he croaked one evening, "I've been here five nights, and I must say I'm very happy. Every morning I go and buy my liter of red, and then I bed down. *Eh bien,* I must say I'm very happy." (Applause.) At the end there was a hard core of about 100, living and sleeping and cooking in the theater, sunbathing on the roof, strutting about as Roman centurions, more like a gang on leave from the street corner and the vacant lot. When the police came on June 14, they all left quietly, giving way to the DDT cleaning squads.

The last days of the Student Soviet were as sad as the first had been heroic. For greater efficiency, perhaps for greater security, the hard-core leaders moved out of the Sorbonne, abandoning it to its fairground role. A group of International Situationists—a latter-day incarnation of surrealism—seized the university loudspeaker system for a time and issued extravagant directives. Worse still, the halls and corridors grew filthy with the shuffling of a thousand feet. Here, too, tramps moved in, and hippies, and people who had nowhere else to sleep. Rats moved up from the sewers; police spies came through the front door. Some youngsters took hashish and needed daily treatment. The infirmary became a scandal. About thirty thugs, petty criminals, ex-Foreign Legionnaires, deserters—calling themselves the *Katangais*—moved into a Sorbonne basement and spread uncertain terror around them. They too, in their way, hated society and had come to help the students, but they brought disrepute. They had a couple of small-bore sports rifles, some ugly-looking knives, a few sticks and bars, some lengths of chain, and a painted girl or two. One night in mid-June there was a scuffle, and they were thrown out by a students' *service d'ordre,* mobilized by the Occupation Committee.

The committee also called for mops and water and disinfectant, to give the vast building a spring cleaning. But it never finished the job. At 2 A.M. on Sunday, June 16, a young man was dumped at the Sorbonne infirmary with a knife wound. The students immediately took him off to the hospital, but a police inquiry followed. Seizing this pretext, the government sent in a force of police which met little resistance. The last teachers and students were driven out singing the "Internationale." Small-scale skirmishing broke out on the boulevards. A few stones were thrown, a few gas grenades. But the student riposte had no sting to it. The red and black flags were hauled down from the Sorbonne and replaced by the Tricolor. One colorful phase of student action was at an end. Having failed to take power, imagination took to the *maquis*. It went underground.

"Sciences Po"

Blanca Camprubi, twenty, a third-year student of the *Institut d'Études Politiques*, reports:

Early in May revision for the final exams had reached its peak. One more little effort, and all those months of work would be rewarded. Revising twelve hours a day, you don't have much time to think about what's going on around you. In any case, politics was never a burning question at the Sciences Po, perhaps because it was on the syllabus; we discussed the great political problems of the world—in the most polished French—but no one thought of importing politics inside the institute. The students were overwhelmingly bourgeois, sons of senior civil servants, of ambassadors, and of distinguished political refugees . . . themselves to become no doubt senior civil servants, ambassadors, and perhaps even distinguished political refugees. Everyone worked very hard and thought only of getting the diploma.

Our working conditions were far better than in the other faculties. For one thing we were only 3,500, and our relations with our teachers were therefore closer than in the Sorbonne. We had an excellent library and a periodicals room which was the envy of the whole university. Some of our lecturers, like Alfred Grosser and André Amar, were extremely popular. But most of our work was done in small groups of fifteen, called *conférences*, where the accent was on learning how to put a case, as clearly and as brilliantly as possible, in exactly ten minutes. This was because a decisive part of our final exam was the oral; one is given an hour to prepare a ten-minute talk on any subject drawn from the whole range of studies. One is then cross-examined for a further ten minutes. Thus the outcome of a whole year's work is decided in exactly twenty minutes and ten seconds. Everyone lived in fear of the oral. There were also worries about careers. For instance, the institute prepares students for entry to the *École Nationale d'Administration,* the gateway into the senior civil service. Five hundred take the exam every year; only about a hundred get through.

But the general tone of Sciences Po is complacent. Students there consider themselves the most intelligent, the best, the most beautiful. This is what needed reform: the state of mind of a small, pretentious, self-satisfied, hard-working, well-dressed community.

On May 3, when the first gas grenades exploded, we were hard at work. We followed the battle until one in the morning—but only over the radio. Someone exclaimed, "It's nice to know we can go on working while the other ranks fight for the cause!" There was no question in that first week of *our* taking part in demonstrations.

Saturday, May 11, was the day we'd all been preparing for; we'd been summoned to start our finals at 8 A.M. But before leaving home, we'd listened to the radio and knew that violence in the Latin Quarter had reached its peak that night and that demonstrations had been called in support of the reopening of the Sorbonne and the freeing of the arrested students. We all met at Chez Basile—the favorite Sciences Po café, around the corner from the school—for a last hurried cup of coffee before the exam. As we came out, we noticed a small crowd at the door of the institute. We knew something was up. Some of the students who had spent the night at the barricades, accompanied perhaps by others from the Sorbonne, had come to ask us to strike in sympathy. There was a moment of doubt, of silence. These were, after all, our final exams. A girl glanced at a boy; there was a pause, then quite suddenly the cry "LIBÉ-REZ NOS CAMA-RADES!" Everyone smiled. The choice was made.

The head of the school, the mysterious and magnificent Jacques Chapsal, appeared. To make himself heard in the bedlam, he had to adopt more democratic methods than he was used to: He climbed on a chair. That day's exam would be postponed, he announced, but all the following ones would take place strictly as planned. Basile, at the door of his café, was astounded to see a mob of students surge past on their way to the demonstration. In ten minutes they had been converted, if not into "wild revolutionaries," at least into "ardent reformers."

As violence spread in the Latin Quarter, even the dullest at the institute realized that we could no longer stand on the sidelines. We had to make up our minds for or against the student movement. The test was a vote organized one night at the school on our attitude to the exams. Groups of professors waited to intercept us at street corners. These lobbies opened our eyes to our own power. A general discussion preceded the vote, and to our astonishment, our revered Professor Alfred Grosser began his remarks with the words "I should like to thank the General Assembly for allowing me to speak."

The vote was taken in an atmosphere of great, but solemn, excitement by secret ballot. The *réacs* (reactionaries) were marshaled against the *révoltes* (rebels). The first proposed that the exams should take place in their present form ten days after the end of the strike which we had called; the second wanted no exams at all. They wanted diplomas to be awarded on the basis of work done during the year, and that time should now be given the students to plan reforms. After heated discussion we dispersed into the street to await the results. Night was falling. Suddenly it came over us that we could speak at the tops of our voices, that we could sing or shout if we wanted to! By a vote, we had undone a year's work; some had even compromised their careers. And yet we experienced a sense of joy far sharper than that of receiving our degrees. The rebels won the vote. That night the permanent occupation of the institute was decided upon. Exams were set aside. The path for reform was open.

We gave ourselves to revolution with all the fervor of late converts. Overnight the Institute of Political Studies of the University of Paris became the Lenin Institute; there was a Che Guevara Hall, a Mao Tse-tung Library, a Rosa Luxemburg Amphitheater. Red and black flags were draped at the entrance. All the manual work was done by the students themselves, and never were the coats so neatly hung in the cloakroom or the lavatory so spotless. Our natures were different from those of our disorderly cousins of the Sorbonne. Our internal planning was faultless under a Committee of Organization, Coordination, and Liaison, even though the slogans on the walls told a different story: "Girls, don't drive men to alienation! Offer yourselves to the revolution!"

But this idyll was interrupted. *Occident*—right-wing students, sworn enemies of all Reds—mounted a commando attack on the school. Helmeted and armed with shields and truncheons, they broke a window in the back of the building and stormed in, sending 500 students at work there fleeing in panic. Some could not escape and rushed upstairs, where they locked themselves in and yelled for help from the windows. Gas grenades, thrown by *Occident,* completed the film. *Occident* closed the iron gates, and the school could only be recaptured by a frontal assault. Our besieged friends in the upper stories threw out chairs, which we broke up to use as weapons. Couriers were sent hotfoot to summon the *service d'ordre* from the Sorbonne—we had

never been on good terms with the faculty of letters, but
at such a moment we needed the help of Big Brother. Our
professor, M. Grosser, took command of the assault.
Hand-to-hand fighting followed, but *Occident,* seeing we
had arms and friends, fled, leaving a prisoner in our hands.
He was locked up in a research student's study, photographed, and numbered. A student tribunal pronounced
sentence: He would be handed over to the police. After
this flurry, we drew up a blacklist of "Fascists," suspected
of collaborating with *Occident.* If they dared return to the
institute, they would be lynched.

To carry out our reforms, we set up elaborate representative bodies. All the *conférences*—the study groups—elected
delegates to a Students' Council, with decision-making
powers. Commissions, open to everyone, debated reforms,
which were then put up to the council. Final decisions were
taken by a council subcommittee of nine students and nine
professors. In the reform commissions, the professors raised
their hands for permission to speak. They were amazed at
the procedural skill of their students.

The current for reform was strong. There was a demand
for political and union freedoms inside the institute, for its
democratization, both regarding student recruitment and
the content of the syllabus. Some students even wanted a
right of veto on the appointment and dismissal of professors. There was an attempt to steer the school away from
its accent on individual performance and toward group
work, away from examination techniques toward a more
profound approach to problems.

But in spite of the red flags and the fiery slogans, the
majority of students were still moderate in temper. It was
as if they understood that without living through this sort
of folly, which gave an emotional reality to what we were
doing, the reforms would be worthless. We had passed the
point of no return. . . .

Les Carabins*

Michel Morin, a second-year medical student, reports:

We are not thought to have sharp, critical minds in the medical faculty, and in May we were rather slow to wake up to what was happening. It's perhaps because medical students soon begin to feel useful in society. They don't have any great career problems. Anyway our studies are so long drawn out and arduous that we don't have much time for politics.

What was extraordinary was the way we, who had hardly raised our noses from our textbooks, were suddenly swept into political activity. Let me give you an example: On May 3 one of my fellow students went to collect his car on the Boulevard St.-Michel. A group of CRS fell on him, beat him up, and called him a "filthy student." A day or two later, when he heard on the radio that fighting had flared up again, he leaped into his car to go and take part. He remembered to take a screwdriver to dislodge the *pavés*. I met him the next morning: He'd become an active rebel—and was even quite articulate about *why* he was fighting.

This sudden political awareness came as a surprise to everyone. On Saturday, May 4, at the end of the anatomy lecture, one of the professors observed rather complacently that at least *we* hadn't taken to the street. But on May 7, when I went back to the faculty, the atmosphere was electric. The walls were covered with posters. The symbols of the revolutionary factions, still unfamiliar to most of the students, were everywhere to be seen. But conservative resistance did not immediately collapse: When a speaker began his address with "Comrades!" there were roars of protest. The first speeches were a bit flatulent—calls for

* The medics.

struggle and vigilance, and so on. I was amazed to discover that one of the most redoubtable orators was a chap whom I knew slightly and whom I'd never suspected of such gifts.

Solidarity with our fellow students was the great mobilizing force. The boys held by the police became symbols. When we heard on the radio the sounds of *pavés* being piled up into barricades, we couldn't help ourselves. The police had to man the bridges to prevent those who lived on the Right Bank rushing to the Latin Quarter. I met other *carabins* at the barricades, and we were astonished to find one another there—so great was our reputation for being political eunuchs.

An organization of student power was immediately set up in the occupied faculty of medicine. Men from each year formed action committees and reported to the General Assembly, which was itself spontaneously formed. Rooms were allotted to committees, and subjects chosen for debate. Of course, at the start, our problem was to decide what to do about the exams. In agreement with the dean it was decided that they should be indefinitely put off and should not be held without six weeks' warning. This was to allow the commissions to get to work and also out of fairness to those who had joined the protest movement from the start. Like other faculties, we set up a *service d'ordre,* helmeted and armed with sticks, guarding our front door to keep out both the police and *Occident*. We also had a team of cleaners—we doctors couldn't afford to be accused of dirt! And of course, there was a first-aid center open on the nights of street warfare. We also set up dormitories, a nursery, and a buffet—where payment was optional. There was a great thirst to run things for ourselves, to tear down the old system whereby the Ministry of Education ran one huge university throughout France. It was really the first time the students felt they were doing something together. But it was also the first time our teachers sat beside us.

They used to be hedged off from us at the center of the amphitheater by a sort of fence; it took the revolution to persuade them to jump over it.

It was fascinating to watch the General Assembly becoming daily more radical, as the moderates tired and gradually gave up. One night, around midnight, someone interrupted a speaker with the cry "Cohn-Bendit is at the Sorbonne!" The hall exploded with joy. Cohn-Bendit, expelled from France, had vowed to return, and in our hearts we all wanted him to bring it off.

Slow to join the student protest, the faculty of medicine was the last in Paris to fly the red flag and finally hauled down by the police at dawn on July 8.

The Cité Universitaire

Rohan Wickramasinghe, twenty-six, a biochemist from Ceylon, reports:

The May conflagration in the Latin Quarter brought in its wake a series of minor bonfires in the Cité Universitaire, a community of residential hostels for some 6,000 mainly foreign students—dignified by the name of national pavilions—on the southern fringe of Paris. As in the faculties, bands of determined men took some of the pavilions by assault and occupied them, in some cases expelling the director and the residents. These occupations, which lasted from five days to six weeks, constitute a comic footnote to the history of the May Revolution. One permanent gain resulted: Sex segregation, long the bane of the Cité, has now gone forever.

Unlike the French protest movement, the Cité insurrections sought neither university reform nor the overthrow of President de Gaulle. They were, almost without exception, gestures of defiance against some distant and allegedly

repressive government. The Greek House was the first to
fall, the new occupants having to defend themselves almost
immediately against a counterattack by a right-wing student
commando. A week later the Spanish House fell to a force
of Spanish students and immigrant workers, supported by
leftist political exiles with memories of the Civil War. It
was immediately renamed the Spanish Workers' and Students' House and was crowded on Sundays with mothers
and children come to wonder at this corner of revolutionary
Spain.

The insurgent movement then spread to the Argentine
Pavilion, promptly renamed Che Guevara House. Tracts,
pamphlets, and posters all testified to the close links the
invaders entertained with Latin American guerrilla groups.
At least twenty of the former residents packed their books
and fled, as the newcomers carried out an ideological spring
cleaning. They uncovered the truly horrifying information
that most of the former inhabitants were over thirty-five,
that some of them made a decent living, and, worst crime of
all, that rooms in the pavilion were allocated in Buenos
Aires on the basis of favoritism or political bias. "This is
not a tourist hotel!" the new militants declared.

The invaders of the Portuguese Pavilion, a gift of the
Gulbenkian Foundation, distinguished themselves by demanding religious, as well as political, freedom. The Mo-
roccans displayed Arab cunning: A group of residents proclaimed the occupation complete, a move, it was rumored,
designed to keep out Algerian workmen. There was no
reason why *this* occupation should ever be brought to
an end.

The Italian occupation, effected by a voluble commando
from Turin, was thrown out after only five days. The Maison d'Indo-Chine was rechristened the Maison du Vietnam
et du Laos, but not before hostilities flared up between
these two nationalities. An assault on the Brazilian House

was repulsed, scaring off, however, the administrative staff; the residents found themselves in unfettered control. The Begian and Swiss houses, the cleanest, quietest, and most prudish of the compound, remained undisturbed.

7 Experiments in Revolution: The Action Committees*

> The Action Committee is the instrument of struggle.
> —LEON TROTSKY

So FAR in our story we have placed in the front rank of the revolutionary leadership a political faction, the JCR; a student union, UNEF; and a mushroom pressure group, Cohn-Bendit's March 22 Movement. But there was another circle of men, more reflective than these, who saw the need for a different sort of mass organization—more flexible, casting its net wider, and yet wholeheartedly committed to revolutionary action. How did this new "instrument of struggle" emerge? The May Revolution was preceded by a whole series of false starts. We showed in Chapter One that the agitation at Nanterre, for example, dated back at least a year. There was no knowing when the tinder would catch fire and a revolutionary situation materialize. When suddenly it did, it took everyone by surprise, including the student leaders. They were no more able to predict and control the headlong course of events than was the government.

Among the most perceptive observers of the situation was a small group of graduate students and research workers, veterans of student politics in the immediate wake of

* We are grateful to Jean Favret and Marc Kravetz for some of the information appearing in this chapter.

Red flag over France.

Snark International/Dumage

Night of the Barricades, May 10–11, 1968.

Snark International/Dumage

Night of the Barricades, May 10–11, 1968.

Student chain gangs building barricades.

Snark International/Chris Marker

Paris riot police on the battlefield.

Ragged police charge.

Snark International/Dumage

Rebel footsoldier in gear filched from Odéon Theater.

Snark International/Ethel

The Student Soviet: Cohn-Bendit at the Sorbonne.

The Student Soviet: the *Grand Amphi* before dawn.

Snark International/Ethel

Snark International/Dufresne

Daybreak on the Boulevard St.-Michel:
dismantling a barricade.

Capitalism on the gallows of an occupied factory.

"Clenched fists for the revolution, comrades":
Renault's home base at Boulogne-Billancourt.

Young strikers on the march.

Snark International/Windenberger

Three faces of France: *(Top)* the proletariat;

(L. below) the Gaullists.

(R. below) the revolutionary young.

Snark International/Lacordaire   *Snark International/Fourmentrau*

Snark International/Chris Marker

"Society is a carnivorous flower."

The demonstration passed this way.

Snark International/Demonestrol

The end of the Student Soviet: sweeping clean the Sorbonne

Alain Geismar (SNESup), Jacques Sauvageot (UNEF)
and Daniel Cohn-Bendit (22 March Movement)
in Paris, May 13, 1968.

Rudi Dutschke and Alain Krivine, the French
JCR leader, in Berlin, February, 1968.

Ewa Rudling

Three A.M. at UNEF headquarters: Jacques Sauvageot.

Barbara Nath

"The Strike Goes On." L'École des Beaux-Arts.

the Algerian War. We have already had occasion to mention them and their political nursery, UNEF's arts section at the Sorbonne, known as the *Fédération des Groupes d'Études de Lettres* (FGEL).* As early as 1963 members of FGEL were formulating fundamental criticisms of the university, attacking it not for its inefficiency but for its role as architect of an inhumane and socially unjust society. These were the themes which were later to echo around the student world, in Berlin, at Columbia, in Rome, and elsewhere. FGEL's early reflection did not bear immediate fruit; the moment was not propitious. But with agitation growing early in 1968, the FGEL veterans were the first to see that a new phase of militant action was opening. At the beginning of March they grouped themselves into the *Mouvement d'Action Universitaire* (MAU) which, as we reported in Chapter Three,† held its first public meeting at the Sorbonne on March 29.††

On May 4, on the morrow of the dramatic events at the Sorbonne, the MAU gathered other likeminded intellectuals —leftists unaffiliated either with UNEF or with political factions such as the JCR—and transformed itself into the *Comités d'Action Universitaire.* A few days later, on May 8, drawing still more people into its net, it became the *Mouvement du 3 Mai,* which was to play a decisive role in the unfolding of events by marching on the Censier faculty of letters and occupying it on Saturday, May 11, the morning after the Night of the Barricades. This was the first occupation of a university building in Paris, the first incarnation of the Student Soviet which ruled over the Latin Quarter for a month.

What did these complicated changes of name reflect? They were the efforts of men who sensed a revolutionary

* See the references to FGEL on pages 46 and 61.
† See page 62.
†† Leading members of the MAU were Marc Kravetz, Jean-Louis Peninou, Brice Lalande, Serge Bosc, and Jean-Marcel Bouguereau. (Bourguereau had been concerned with UNEF's foreign relations and in this capacity made early contacts with German students.)

potential in the fast-moving situation, and were groping for an "instrument of struggle" to harness this potential. It seemed to them that Marxism had ceased to be purely verbal and could now be clad in flesh and blood. From their university standpoint, they understood that the revolt which was sweeping France was not a contest for executive power in the classical sense; nor was it an uprising of despair springing from economic crisis. It was a thirst for liberty at every level of life, an urge to throw off the cramping cant and petty tyranny of fossilized institutions. It was what the French call a *crise de structures*—something quite new, perhaps the first rebellion against the way twentieth-century capitalism is organized. These intellectuals suffocated in the worm-eaten framework of French bourgeois values and culture patterns. They wanted to break this mold and throw out a bridge to the workers, to rediscover the common ground of intellectual and manual effort. However incoherently and inadequately expressed here, these were the seminal ideas of the May Revolution. This was what the militants were groping for when they spoke of turning the Sorbonne into a *université critique* and a *université populaire*. But if the energies released by the revolt were not to be dissipated, they had to be worked upon, regulated, channeled into purposeful political directions. Hence the need for new institutions. To conceive, set up, and control these institutions was from start to finish the major problem facing the young leaders. The success or failure of the revolution depended on it.

The *comité d'action* was the vehicle chosen by the revolutionary leadership to mobilize mass support for its aims. It was, as we suggested in Chapter Five, an old idea, a variant of the councils which mushroom in most revolutions, basic self-governing units diametrically opposed to the topheavy bureaucratic apparatus of the modern state. The occupation of Censier on May 11 launched the movement. The hard-core militants of the *Mouvement du 3 Mai* soon gained support from the JCR, from men who were active in the *Comité Vietnam National,* even from the pro-Chinese UJC(M-L) people, who, in fact, had already set up on their own account a string of Defense Committees Against Repression. All these joined forces to inspire a flourishing of *comités d'action* right across Paris. They sprang up with incredible speed, in schools, universities, government offices, professional organizations, and firms, but also spontaneously in residential areas on the basis of a network of streets. These *comités* were in many cases no more than groups of active citizens, usually between ten and fifty strong, unaffiliated for the most part with any particular political movement. What they had in common in those uncertain, delirious May days when the Gaullist state seemed to be melting away was the idea that revolution is something you do yourself, not something you leave to others. They were the expression of a will for direct, extra-parliamentary action. They declared themselves ready to "pass from spontaneous violence to the preparation of organized violence." This was one of the slogans at the movement's General Assembly on May 19, held in the Institut d'Art et d'Archéologie on the Rue Michelet, at which no fewer than 250 action committees were represented. There was, of course, something unreal and romantic in these words of violence in the mouths of the humane, intelligent economists, sociologists, university teachers, and housewives there gathered. But there was no mistaking their intense concern for the future of French society.

The movement reached its peak in the last week of May, when there were at least 450 action committees in Paris alone. Taken together, they formed a remarkably flexible and effective instrument in the hands of the revolutionary leaders who exerted some control over these far-flung cells through a Coordinating Committee. This met daily for two weeks in the Sorbonne after its occupation, then moved to the Institute of Psychology in the Rue Serpente, where, at the time of writing, it still was.

The *comités d'action* enjoyed considerable local autonomy and engaged in an enormous variety of tasks. Some preferred down-to-earth practical work, like collecting money for strikers' families, or clearing away rubbish, which piled high at street corners during the crisis, or ferrying people around in cars when transportation had collapsed. In this way they acted like a new sort of municipal authority—a classic example of the *double pouvoir* which springs up at moments of crisis. Other *comités d'action* behaved more like the cells of a political movement: They wrote tracts and distributed them; they made posters and pasted them up on walls; they buttonholed passersby and organized street meetings; they showed films and exhibited photographs of police brutality. Their daily aim was to mobilize larger and larger numbers of people in the revolutionary struggle against the Gaullist regime. Organization and agitation were thus the two poles between which the *comités d'action* oscillated. These differences in conception and function, as well as the strong local bias of each committee, made the movement as a whole difficult to control.

Another element of confusion was that existing political parties, seeing the success of the action committees, attempted to do likewise. The Communist Party inspired a number of Action Committees for a Government of the People and Democratic Union,* while the *Parti Socialiste Unifié,* a splinter group on the extreme left of democratic Socialism, set up a number of *Comités d'Action Populaires.* But neither of these achieved anything like the extension of the original movement.

When General de Gaulle made his comeback and triumphed at the elections of June 23 and June 30, the action committees were naturally somewhat deflated. Revolution

* *Comités d'Action pour un Gouvernement Populaire et d'Union Democratique.*

seemed no longer around the corner. Some groups simply disintegrated, their members shaking their heads at their moment of folly. But many *comités* are still active. They are convinced that DeGaulle could have been overthrown in that last week of May had there existed in France a political movement ready to step into the breach. They want to avoid the mistakes of May and prepare for a second round. In hard-boiled political terms, these sentiments may be utopian nonsense, but they reflect the disturbing fact that many French men and women no longer believe that the ills of their society can be cured by peaceful and parliamentary means. Power, they say, is in the street.

8 Experiments in Revolution: The Teen-Age Army*

> A good *lycée* is one which teaches patricide.
>
> A SCHOOLBOY

ONE of the most astonishing sights of the May Revolution was thousands of schoolchildren marching to the slogan "Power is in the street, not in Parliament!" This is a phenomenon to make any Western government tremble; it is nothing less than the rejection by the elite of the rising generation of the political institutions and values of its parents. Radical ideas are sweeping through French *lycées* at a speed unknown in adult politics, transforming the tone of French school life, the relations between teachers and pupils, even the content of the syllabus. The forbidding barrackslike buildings still look the same, but they have been captured from the inside by teen-age insurgents. This revolt has attracted less attention than that of the older boys and girls at university, but it is as thoroughgoing and, if anything, more significant for the future. Moreover, the schoolchildren are organized for revolution in a way their elder brothers and sisters are not yet; the vehicle is the *Comité d'Action Lycéen* (CAL).

It is no surprise to discover that the Vietnam War—and the protest movement organized against it in France—lie at the root of this adolescent militancy. Like the Algerian War before it, but still more powerfully, it drew young minds to

---

* We are grateful to Michel Recanati, seventeen, of the Lycée Jacques Decour, for some of the information in this chapter.

politics. From December, 1966, a string of *Comités Vietnam Lycéens* (CVL's—school Vietnam committees—were set up across France. They were for the most part small groups of up to 30 young people—in *lycées* of up to 3,000 —who had fallen out with the French Communist Party's schools organization, the *Mouvement de la Jeunesse Communiste* (MJC), because they thought the CPF's Vietnam policy too tame. The CVL's provided the infrastructure on which the CAL's were to be built, moving beyond Vietnam protest to action in France directed against specifically French problems.

This phase began in December, 1967. The principal French trade unions and UNEF, the students' union, called a strike on December 13 to protest against government decrees cutting Social Security benefits. To everyone's surprise, half a dozen Paris *lycées* struck in sympathy—the first such strike in France. Strike pickets were formed by CVL militants, who brought their schoolfellows out with slogans referring exclusively to school problems; the leaders knew well they would not be followed on a call for solidarity with the workers. Needless to say, the authorities, shaken by the strike, moved in to crush the leaders. In January, 1968, sixteen-year-old Romain Goupil, who had organized a picket at the Lycée Condorcet, was expelled on the charge that he had incited his comrades to skip class, but what really offended the headmaster was his political agitation. Goupil, a member of the JCR, distributed Trotskyist propaganda in school, held discussions, and was generally a fount of revolutionary ideas. Immediately, from *lycée* to *lycée,* the CVL leaders consulted one another by telephone about their riposte. They decided to call on their comrades to demonstrate—once again, the first time *lycéens* had ever done so. Several hundred turned up and marched to the slogan of "Freedom of expression in the *lycées*"—a line which the leaders correctly believed would be easily understood. This was the birth of the CAL's.

The next test was on February 26, when French secondary schoolteachers struck for better conditions. The CAL's at once organized strike pickets in support of the teachers, advancing at the same time their own claims. That same night 600 schoolboys and girls gathered to discuss what should be the future role of their embryonic organization. It was an important meeting. For the first time school militancy was linked to left-wing political objectives. The leaders presented a report claiming that education was a slave to the economic system. Words like "capitalist" and "Socialist" were used. It was suggested that the role of the CAL's was to denounce the education system as an instrument of social selection. The idea was to challenge society by challenging the school. This was as far as they had got by April, 1968—still a small movement in a handful of *lycées,* affecting about 500 schoolchildren.

The street fighting on May 3, following the police invasion of the Sorbonne, had a shattering effect on adolescents. In many *lycées* there were immediate strikes. Classes were interrupted as young people abandoned their work to discuss the situation. Many rushed to join the demonstrations; some were wounded. On May 10 the CAL's called an all-day strike in all Paris *lycées,* and a teen-age force, some 8,000 to 9,000 strong, marched to join their seniors in the great demonstration which ended at the barricades. What propaganda had failed to do in a year, action did in three hours. A long tradition of schoolboy passivity was broken. The CAL's had preached that the pressures of home, school, and police were all faces of the same repression. At the barricades that night the lesson was rammed home. Faced with the choice at midnight of going home to Mommy or staying out all night to fight, many chose to stay. From then on the *lycéens* were never absent from the front line.

Once the Sorbonne was occupied, the CAL's took over the *Grand Amphithéâtre* for their General Assembly on

May 19. It was then that they decided on the next crucial step—a general strike and the occupation of the schools. The next day the movement was widely followed, with teachers in some cases joining in and spending the night on the premises. Committees were formed to discuss not only school and university problems, but also politics: subjects like student struggles in Europe, the role of the university in society, student-worker links, and so on. Here, as in other sectors of French life, the revolution brought an extraordinary explosion of talk. Thousand of young people who had never had a political idea in their lives were drawn in. Parents came to watch and wonder. Teachers found themselves arguing with their students with an interest they had never had in class. Workers were invited in to see Russian films. The general tone was intensely serious, more so than at university level. There was none of the libertine anarchy of the Sorbonne. Instead, earnest committees sat late and drafted reports, largely on school reform. No fewer than 300 were produced in the last fortnight of May.

The CAL's emerged from the revolution as a force in French national education. Their advice was sought—unofficially—on the subject of the *baccalauréat,* which this year, because of the crisis, was restricted to a brief oral exam. Another pointer to their power is that their right to put up political posters in the schools is no longer contested. Large numbers of schoolchildren have become politically aware. But the future role of the CAL's is still in doubt and, at the time of writing, is the subject of intense debate. Should they be an extreme left-wing revolutionary pressure group? Or should they seek to be a sort of schoolboy union, spokesmen for everyone's interests? The present leadership is wholly against this second course, but neither does it want the CAL's to be identified as an extremist political faction. They see themselves not as a political organization directed against De Gaulle's regime, but rather as an avant-garde leading French adolescents to political awareness. They believe in education through action, not through propaganda. This is the main lesson they have drawn from the month of May.

The CAL's have proved so successful that both the Communists and the Gaullists are trying to set up rival youth organizations in the schools. The Communists packed the mid-June national conference of the CAL's and took over the meeting, forming their own National Union of School Action Committees. The Gaullists have founded a National Union of French Lycées and Colleges. Both hope to limit the influence of the CAL's by being apolitical and reformist.

But the CAL's have plans which should keep the *lycées* in the political front line. Their attack will be twofold: first, short-term and institutional; second, long-term and more fundamental. In the short term, they are aiming for a share in decision making inside the schools. French *lycées* are run by a *conseil intérieur,* on which sit the *proviseur,* who is the Ministry of Education representative; the *censeur,* a sort of director of studies; and the teachers. Only the *proviseur* can make decisions. The role of the others is purely consultative. The CAL's want to get a seat on the *conseil intérieur* and to secure with the teachers a real measure of power. In the longer run, they have a vision of turning the *lycées* into cultural and political centers for the whole neighborhood: They want to take them out of their present intellectual ghetto; they want to throw them open to the workers for debates and cultural activities. The boys and girls do not want to fight their teachers, but to bring them over to their point of view. Whatever happens, there will be no going back.

9 Experiments in Revolution: The Liberal Professions

Le football aux footballeurs

IF proof were needed that the events of May amounted to a revolution, the profound upheaval which then took place in the liberal professions provides it. This was not a movement of a handful of *enragés;* no sinister foreign hand could here be suspected. The rebels were doctors, men of law, churchmen; journalists and film makers; artists, musicians, painters, and writers; social scientists and statisticians; archivists, librarians, and astronomers; atomic scientists and museum directors. They were the intellectual backbone of the country, and in their thousands they rose to challenge the *structures* which governed their work. They rebelled, that is, against excessive centralization, poor delegation of power, against the mandarins, satraps, and *grands patrons* who until May ruled over French professional life. Inevitably the professions most immediately affected were those with close links with the university, but the virus soon spread very much farther afield. The vaunted Gaullist order cloaked, it appears, an immense and generalized disorder.

The Doctors

Some weeks before the revolution France's first heart transplant cast a sharp light on the outdated power structure of the French medical profession. The operation was carried out at La Pitié Hospital in Paris, in a department of heart surgery, headed by a Professor Cabrol. But when news of the patient was given to the French public in what seemed almost hourly TV communiqués, the chief spokesman was a Professor Mercadier. As the French satirical newspaper *Le Canard Enchaîné* was the first to reveal, Mercadier had not been in Paris at the time of the operation and was in any event a specialist in the surgery, not of the heart, but of the digestive tract. But he was the *grand patron* of La Pitié. Here was exposed the system in all its antique absurdity. As head of the hospital, Professor Mercadier alone bore full moral, administrative, and legal responsibility for everything that went on in his hospital. If owing to negligence or criminality, a patient in any of the hospital's 140-beds were to suffer, he would have to take the blame. He also took the credit for any medical successes. His subordinates, department heads like Professor Cabrol, however distinguished, enjoyed absolutely no powers of independent decision. *Structures* 100 years old had not been adapted to take into account the specialization of modern medicine.

No wonder then that May found the medical profession ready for revolution. Everywhere empires started to crumble, but particularly in the teaching hospitals. The great cry was for decentralization, collective leadership, promotion on the basis of talent, rather than age. We cannot here give an account of the furious debate which overtook the whole medical profession in the last two weeks of May, 1968, and which is certain to result in a thorough reorganization of teaching and responsibilities. One landmark is perhaps noteworthy, if only to demonstrate that revolutionaries were to be found at the top of the profession, as well as in the wards. On May 20 Dean Brouet of the faculty of medicine of Paris called on the whole medical teaching staff to approve this program: (1) recognition of student power in teaching hospitals; (2) the autonomy of teaching hospitals; (3) remuneration for medical students for work done in hospitals; (4) abolition of professorial chairs and their replacement by departments under team direction.

Some general practitioners, notably the bureaucracy running the Domus Medica, home of the National Council of Doctors, were not so liberal. They came under violent attack, and their offices were occupied by an action committee, which had finally to be expelled with the help of the police. But the profession will never be again the dignified, rather stuffy thing it was.

The Church

In early June, 1968, shortly after General de Gaulle had checked the tide of revolution, a young curate in the south of France was involved in a painful scene. The Abbé Charles-Guy de Kérimel was delivering his Sunday sermon in the middle-class parish of St.-Jean-de-Malte in Aix-en-Provence when there were shouts and catcalls from the congregation. About forty people got up and left the church. What had he said that was so offensive? He had remarked that the workers on strike throughout France were perhaps in search of human dignity and that there was "something a little indecent" about the sigh of relief which had followed the collapse of the revolution. The abbé was just one of the many Catholics who came to believe— and said so in public—that the May Revolution had lessons for the church. Here too were fossilized institutions, mandarins, obstacles to free and fruitful communication not only between priests and people, but also within the ecclesiastical hierarchy. The malaise was recognized by Monseigneur Marty, the new Archbishop of Paris, a modest and humane cleric. He visited the Latin Quarter during the fighting and, in a diocesan letter, expressed understanding for the rebels' rejection of a consumer and materialistic society: "God stands for justice; He is not a conservative," he wrote. "Some belated reforms are now imperative. Christians too must challenge a society which neglects the profound aspirations of man." This struck a chord among the young, whom it encouraged to criticize all the more vigorously the lifeless fare other churchmen gave them on Sunday. At a marathon debate organized at the university chaplaincy, there were demands for "a Christian revolution." One seminarian, who had fled his seminary to come to Paris for the discussions said, "I felt it more important to come to testify here than to go on comparing Genesis One with Psalm One Hundred and Four as I'd been doing for the last week."

Left-wing Catholicism has been a source of progressive and radical thinking in France for a generation. It has fertilized political and intellectual circles but has often bypassed the church itself. But one parish which last spring could hardly escape revolutionary contagion was St.-Séverin, in the heart of the Latin Quarter. On Whitsunday early last June, a few minutes before the ten o'clock mass began, the church was invaded by banner-bearing young Catholics. "We want to reinvent the church!" they cried. Failing to persuade the priest to substitute a debate for mass, they waited for the parishioners outside and later kept them from their lunch in long discussions in the cloisters.

Some dozen young Jews invaded the premises of the Jewish "Consistory" and issued a statement contesting the archaic and nondemocratic structures of their community institutions.

Protestant theological students were even more revolutionary, going on strike in Paris and Montpellier and declaring that the church was an "alienating, self-perpetuating society. So much we learned at the barricades!" The Paris rebels signed their communiqué "Students of the (so-called) Free Faculty of Protestant Theology."

The Creative Arts

The May Revolution set off an angry ferment in the arts which would need a book to do it justice. We have space for only one or two points: This was not a limited phenomenon but one affecting musicians, painters, film makers, actors, writers, and countless others, and it was a revolt not of the lunatic fringe but of the best young men at work in France today. Thirty directors of provincial theaters and Maisons de la Culture—Culture Minister André Malraux's multi-purpose arts centers—met for a whole week at the height of the crisis in May pondering what should be France's cultural policy of the future. It is to Malraux's credit that these men are on the whole leftish non-Gaullists. But the joint statement they issued was a sharp indictment of the minister's pet scheme of bringing the arts to the provinces. To a man they wanted a far more radical program than the government's highbrow cultural colonies provide. "We must get at the 'non-public,' " they declared, "and draw it out of its ghetto." They made a bid for socially committed art—cultural action should give people a chance to discover their humanity repressed by the absurdity of the social system.

Painters, critics, and gallery directors formed an action committee for the plastic arts. One day in May some of them decided to march on the National Museum of Modern Art and close it down in protest against its role of "conservation, rather than lively encounter." They got there to find the doors locked, so they pasted up a poster saying, "Closed because Useless." Artists met trade unionists to discuss exhibiting their work in factories. Inflamed by the thought of creating a *Maison de la Culture* in a workshop, among the lathes and the steam hammers, they sent paintings to be hung at Nord-Aviation's plant near Paris. This was one of several spirited, if somewhat ineffectual, attempts to bridge the gap between an elite public and the workers; a striking factory near Grenoble was the scene of an Arnold Wesker play.

The May Revolution unfolded against a background of recorded pop music interrupted every half hour on Radio Luxembourg and Europe Number One by news flashes from the barricades. One of the victims was serious music. *France Musique,* the day long classical music program on the French state radio, was silent; all the principal orchestras were on strike. Not only instrumentalists but also composers and arrangers and orchestrators struck in sympathy with the insurgent students of the Latin Quarter. But almost immediately the strikers focused their attention on their own grievances in the musical world, such as the stinginess of radio time given to young composers and the small say that opera singers have in deciding what they sing. Everyone in the small, disorganized, divided world of French music was agreed on the need for a more liberal state cultural policy, but most recognized that the root of the problem was the deplorable way music and indeed all the arts was taught in France. A Committee for the Preparation of a Reform of Artistic Teaching held a marathon debate from mid-May far into June, drawing in students, teachers, and artists in all fields. What they proposed was nothing less than the creation of a university of the arts, which, they agreed, would mean the complete transformation of existing schools, if not their abolition. They complained of the watertight compartments into which art was slotted, of the way teaching foundered in old-fashioned ruts cut off from living art. They demanded that artistic education be an essential part of general education. Allowing their imagination full rein, they spoke even of a ministry of music, defending the interests of music throughout the country. Can the authorities long ignore such a rebellion by a whole profession?

The closing of the Cannes Film Festival was another

and more spectacular pointer to the wave of self-analysis that overtook the world of art in May. More privately and more constructively, about 1,300 people in the film industry met regularly in Paris for nearly a month from May 17 onward in the so-called States General of the French Cinema. They split into working parties, drafted reports, prepared a "charter" for the renovation of the whole industry. At the root of these ambitious plans was the feeling that the French cinema was cut off from the social and political realities of the country. Some young directors blamed the caution of producers and backers; others, government censorship or the threat of a ban if a film touched too directly on official policy; still others blamed themselves and the rigidities of a class structure which made them strangers to working-class life. All blamed the "system." But the charter was too utopian a document to survive; it ran counter to the economic facts of film production. Instead, the States General approved a program of proposed reforms, perhaps the most important of which were the creation of a single national film-distributing organization; the setting up of autonomous production groups freed from the pressures of the profit motive; the doing away with censorship; and the merger of television and moviehouse film production. These are expressions of hope, rather than practical expectations. But one battle is already engaged: that of showing the French public—free from censorship or government ban—the many short films inspired by the extraordinary days of May.

On May 21 a literary commando—comprising the novelists Michel Butor and Nathalie Sarraute and a dozen other writers—invaded and occupied the dignified Paris headquarters of the Society of Men of Letters, thus striking a symbolic blow, as they declared, at a "decayed and unrepresentative institution." They announced the foundation of a Union of Writers, "open to all those who believe that the practice of literature is indissolubly linked with the present revolutionary process." Very soon some fifty other writers, including Sartre, Beauvoir, and Marguerite Duras, declared their support. At the start, relations between the new revolutionary union and the Men of Letters were amicable. The newcomers were even offered a small room. But their ranks were soon swollen by a lively crowd of students from the Sorbonne, followed by members of an anarchist federation, who, it was feared, would make their occupation "permanent." Soon there were three or four rival occupying factions, and argument broke out between the students and the anarchists. The Men of Letters were driven out.

The newly formed union survived these trials and a week later held its first General Assembly, attended by about 200 literary figures, translators, students, and foreigners. The three-hour debate that followed was scarcely more illuminating than the discussions which had raged earlier that week on such subjects of burning interest as Marx, Lenin, and the status of a writer in a Socialist society. The General Assembly finally came to the conclusion that the object of the union was "to define itself in defining the writer." It threw itself open to all those who wished to contest the established economic and social order and to take part in building a new society based on common ownership of the means of production and their democratic management. It was not until the end of July that the Men of Letters recovered their state-owned building after long and, it must be said, acrimonious negotiations.

Other Protesters

French lawyers have traditionally been deeply embroiled in politics—and not only in Parliament, where, until the elections in June, 1968, they constituted the largest single group. They are prominent on the right of the spectrum, with such fiery spirits as Maître Tixier-Vignancour, and on the left, with a phalanx of "committed" jurists always ready to spring to the defense of victims of police repression at home or colonial repression abroad, as during the Algerian War. Not unnaturally, relations between these groups reached a point only just short of armed conflict during May, particularly on May 22, when wild rumors spread through the Palais de Justice in Paris of an imminent student assault. The right, marshaled under the redoubtable Tixier-Vignancour, were there, ready to take on the revolutionaries. But the day ended with nothing more blood-letting than a battle of communiqués. More serious developments, however, were afoot in the profession. Numerous legal bodies met to take stock of the situation—to contest the often stumbling administration of the law and to issue declarations, whose burden was the need for thoroughgoing reforms giving the judiciary real independence from the executive. To press this claim, 150 young magistrates met on June 8 to found a professional union—itself a revolutionary step in French legal tradition.

There was no end to the contesters. At the postgraduate École Nationale d'Administration—the tough nursery of senior bureaucrats, whose graduates form a powerful old-boy network at key posts in the French civil service—the 1967–69 class decided by a majority vote to call itself the Class of Jean Jaurès, the French Socialist leader who founded *L'Humanité* and was killed by an assassin's bullet at the outbreak of the First World War. This was their discreet way of taking sides. (A strong minority was in favor of calling themselves the Class of the People's Spring.)

Astronomers at Meudon Observatory examined the *structures* of their research centers and found them wanting; 200 museum curators from all over France met to ponder the role of museums in society, while their staffs "at one with the great movement of renovation now sweeping the country," called for an overhaul of old-fashioned, sterile, overcentralized museum administration. Christian Fouchet, then Minister of the Interior and a main target for the revolutionaries' anger was himself a victim of the wave of occupations. He happened to live in a vast, two-floor, state-owned apartment looking out over Paris from the roof of the Musée de l'Homme, center of French ethnographic research, which was cramped for space. On May 25 seven high-powered ethnographers and department heads scaled the railing separating the museum terrace from that of M. Fouchet and informed Mme. Fouchet that they had come to take over the apartment on behalf of the museum. She telephoned her husband. A quarter of an hour later the police arrived and carried off the scientists to a detention center near Vincennes, where after interrogation they were released that night. (It is thought that the minister, who lost his job in the crisis, later gave a pledge to vacate the apartment.)

Architects, statisticians, journalists, and librarians were overtaken by the same rebellious fever. Even footballers could not fail to be moved by the spirit of the time. About a hundred of them occupied the seat of the French Football Federation, on the Avenue d'Iéna on May 22, hoisted the red flag from the balcony, locked up the secretary-general and the national instructor, and hung a banner over the façade saying, *Le football aux footballeurs!*

"La Police à l'ORTF c'est la Police Chez Vous"

The abortive struggle of May, 1968, for a free and objective radio and television service could stand as a symbol for what the revolution was about. It was a revolt against political bosses, against excessive centralization, against petty regulations, against a remote and often ignorant bu-

---

* "The police at the TV station means the police in your home" —this was the message on a revolutionary poster.
    We are grateful to Graham Lovell for some of the information in this section.

reaucracy which took decisions without consulting those most concerned. The stage management of events and information is an essential element in President de Gaulle's style of government. No strike last spring caused the regime more fury and in no sector was it more eager to reassert its authority than in the ORTF—Office de la Radio et Télévision Française.

As in so many other sectors of intellectual life, this was not a strike about wages, working conditions, or trade union rights. It was a strike for the complete overhaul of the ORTF's 1964 statute and its replacement by a new charter guaranteeing internal autonomy, freedom from ministerial pressures, and an impartial news service to include freer access to radio and TV for opposition politicians. What united all but 2,000 of the 14,000 employees was, in the words of one of them, "shame"—shame that when fighting broke out in the Latin Quarter, the state television service, under government pressure, ignored it. Pressure of this sort was no new thing for the ORTF, although its use had never seemed so blatant. It was exercised routinely through a committee called the Service de Liaison Interministériel pour l'Information (SLI). At daily meetings of the SLI the director of television outlined scheduled news and feature programs to representatives of government departments, who suggested revisions, additions, or deletions. The SLI was one of the first victims of the prestrike agitation at the ORTF.

Oddly enough government control of radio was never as firm as of television, and France-Inter—the round-the-clock French home service—came into its own during the troubles with coverage of the Latin Quarter on a par with the front-line reporting of the two commercial stations, Radio Luxembourg and Europe Number One. Indeed, one Cabinet minister described France-Inter as "Peking Radio," so fair and sympathetic was its coverage of the students' revolt. But this moment of freedom was short-lived, and the radio newsroom soon followed television into the long strike. Breaking point for the ORTF came with a controversy over the screening of a film on the student riots— the centerpiece of a thrice-monthly TV program called *Panorama*—due to be shown on May 10. *Panorama* is produced and shot entirely by the ORTF staff, unlike three other popular documentary shows—*Zoom, Camera III,* and *Cinq Colonnes à la Une*—made by outside crews. The government stopped the *Panorama* film but allowed a *Zoom* program which included interviews with Daniel Cohn-Bendit and other student leaders to run a few days later. The *Zoom* staff had made it clear that if their show were banned, they would suspend production indefinitely. The ORTF men protested at the seeming injustice of one law for the outsiders and another for them. They were further affronted when a doctored *Panorama* program, including old and by then outdated interviews, was screened. The TV journalists were near to striking at this point, but they held their horses when the government allowed television cameras into the National Assembly for the censure debate of May 21–22. For the first time in years the French public was allowed to see what a free television service could do.

This truce between journalists and their government bosses ended when, with the crisis approaching its peak, General de Gaulle appeared on television on Friday, May 24, to announce his proposed referendum. On the eve of the speech TV journalists, on their own initiative, invited Gaullists and opposition politicians to watch the President's address from the studio and stand by to make immediate comments. When TV Director General Emile Biasini heard of the plan on Friday afternoon, he "almost exploded out of his chair," as one journalist recalled. But the guests were already on their way to the studio, and the first to arrive was Gaston Defferre, a leader of the Federation of the Left, Socialist mayor of Marseilles, and proprietor of one of the biggest Mediterranean coast newspapers. All was confusion at the studio. M. Biasini told the assembled guests that their comments could not go out that evening because the schedule was already full; they would be broadcast the following night. This was reported in the Saturday morning press, but an hour before the scheduled broadcast the program was scrapped on orders from Jacques-Bernard Dupont, ORTF director general. Ninety minutes later the TV journalists were on strike. The France-Inter newsroom did not join them for another week. In the meantime they continued desultory negotiations with the government, described by one of them as "an aimless exercise in rhetoric in which neither side was on the same wavelength."

On May 31 M. Pompidou reshuffled his Cabinet, and Georges Gorse, the luckless Minister of Information during the crisis, was replaced by a younger man, Yves Guéna, who was brought in from the Ministry of Posts and Telegraphs. Guéna behaved as if radio and television were just another public service like the mails. He called in a delegation and gave them the government's terms: no change in the 1964 statute (this could be done only by Parliament, and the Assembly was now dissolved); no change in the way senior appointments were made; no *comité des sages*— the independent three-man council which the journalists wanted to pronounce on allegations of partiality or bias in the ORTF's news handling. He did, however, say that the government would set up a commission to examine the journalists' demands. He gave the men until midnight to consider his proposals. "It was a typical Gaullist take-it-or-leave-it deal," one journalist said. "No wonder there used to be trouble in the Post Office."

At 7 P.M. that evening M. Guéna's offer was broadcast on France-Inter. With a nice sense of drama, the newscaster put down the minister's communiqué, picked up his own, and declared: "Having heard the minister's statement, the joint radio trade unions have decided to strike." The ORTF was strike-bound.

Police had already been posted around the Maison de la Radio on the Avenue Président Kennedy, with heavy reinforcements of CRS manning the side streets. This force seemed to the strikers less a protection than a threat. Large sections of the public did not grasp what the strike was about and were, if anything, hostile to a movement which was starving them of their favorite programs. The second television channel was off the air, while Channel One made do with a single nightly news program clumsily put together by inexperienced men or old-timers brought back from retirement. Radio was a dull fare of taped music punctuated by hourly news bulletins. To win over the public to their cause, the strikers, deprived of their own medium, turned to the stage. They put on shows in thirty provincial towns and ten Parisian and suburban theaters. Well-known performers toured France as a traveling circus. It was an indication of the country's mood that the public seemed less interested in the stars than in the discussions that followed the performances. It wanted less monologue and more dialogue. A TV journalist reported that in one provincial town: "We were approached by two elderly and eminently respectable gentlemen, both wearing the ribbon of the Legion of Honor, 'You are Communists and troublemakers, and we shall say as much in the hall!' they told us. But they didn't. They kept us talking until two A.M., and when the theater finally closed, knocked up the best restaurant in town to give us dinner." In Paris the strike committee organized daily parades around the broadcasting house in what they called Operation Jericho.

To the end the journalists maintained that their strike was not a political act; they were against all government pressure, not just that of the Gaullist regime. As one of them put it, "General de Gaulle must now grant independence to this last French colony." There was a drift back to work, accompanied by fear of reprisals against the strikers. It had been the most dignified and the longest of all spring's strikes. But it had failed. The minister had the last word. "We've got to take some of the drama out of this question of objectivity," he remarked.

10 The Great Strike

FROM mid-May to mid-June, 1968, France lay inert in the chains of a great strike. It was the biggest labor revolt in French history, and it ended in a political fiasco. Why? Historians will long debate the paradox of how a movement involving nearly 10,000,000 workers—politically roused and determined as never before—ended with an overwhelming Gaullist victory at the polls. Was the revolution bungled or betrayed? Was it an illusion, or did the advanced Western world miss by a hairsbreadth its first successful proletarian uprising?

So far, in this book, we have talked mainly of students, schoolboys, and professional men. The moment has now come to be "serious," as a Frenchman might say. Had the workers not joined the nationwide protest movement, the events of May would have had no more—and no less—significance than the student explosions of Berlin, Rome, or Buenos Aires. What distinguishes the French situation from that of other countries is that here the students' example was immediately and massively copied, carrying the crisis to a new level of gravity. From one end of France to another, men and women in key industries seized their places of work and closed the gates. For the first time in recent history intellectuals and manual workers seemed to be marching side by side to revolution. And yet President de Gaulle's regime survived. In spite of the factory occupations, the working class in its immense majority did not cross that fateful frontier between striking for higher wages, shorter working hours, earlier retirement—all the traditional claims—and striking to change society. In isolated plants the movement went further. Some strike committees became so well organized as to seem the expression of a new form of workers' power. As in the student movement, there were among the strike leaders both reformists and revolutionaries, those who thought in terms of wage packages and union rights and those who had a mystical vision of a workers' state. But whatever young revolutionaries may claim, there is no full-scale chapter to be written on "Experiments in Revolution" in the French working class in 1968. We are writing with some hindsight; to the politicians, trade unionists, youth leaders, who fought, plotted, and dreamed in those extraordinary May days, the outcome was not so predictable. Anything seemed possible: the fall of De Gaulle; civil war; a government of the people. We shall try in this chapter briefly to reconstruct the way the French crisis, after the somber Night of the Barricades of May 10–11, entered a new phase, leaping like a spark from students to workers and back again, setting off a chain reaction of explosions, each nourished by the other.

No one is absolutely certain how the great strike started. There is no easy explanation why men, driven to the limits of exasperation, suddenly lay down their tools, like an act of war. The reader will remember from Chapter Four that M. Pompidou returned from Afghanistan on the night of May 11 and single-handedly completely reversed government policy toward the insurgent students. Repression gave way to appeasement. Force—the weapon of last resort—had been used in his absence and had failed. Pompidou saw that no choice but a dignified climb-down was open to him. He sought to secure by inertia what truncheons and tear gas had failed to deliver. He decided to give the students enough rope to hang themselves. But the execution of this policy required great nerve; it meant playing weak, giving free rein to the rebels, abandoning the Latin Quarter to them, and hoping that their violence and anarchistic excesses would soon win back to the government that measure of public support required to strike them down. Pompidou had the guts and authority to impose this policy on General de Gaulle and risk his career on its success. This was the policy he skillfully presented to the National Assembly on Tuesday, May 14. He held out his hand to the students. "Everything," he declared with a touch of disarming contrition, "must be rethought." *Le Monde* commented ironically: "It was a delight to hear the strong man of the government vaunt the merits of dialogue and participation."

This was the situation when General de Gaulle left France that same Tuesday for a state visit to Rumania. He was confident that M. Pompidou—the dauphin to whom he had entrusted his constitutional powers—would soon reduce the crisis to manageable proportions. Did the President imagine that the disturbances could be confined to the university? A year earlier he had been forced to put off a planned visit to Rumania. He did not wish to do it again. But in retrospect, his decision to leave Paris at such a time seems scarcely credible. On the eve of his departure, 800,-000 workers and students paraded through Paris in the biggest demonstration the capital had witnessed for years. To a generation which had not seen the Liberation, let alone the upheavals of 1936, Monday, May 13, was a stupendous landmark, the sealing of a revolutionary alliance against the Gaullist state. That night the Sorbonne was occupied, and the Student Soviet launched on its delirious course, under the gaze of workers, as well as students everywhere. The watertight compartments had been breached. Within hours of General de Gaulle's arrival in Bucharest, workers in a small aircraft plant on the outskirts of Nantes struck and occupied their factory and locked the manager in his office.

Quite independently that Tuesday some workshops at a Renault plant manufacturing gearboxes at Cléon, near Rouen, downed tools. On Wednesday some 200 young strikers tried to get the night shift to join them, but failed, so they barricaded themselves inside the works. When the morning shift arrived at 5 A.M. on Thursday, May 16, they found the doors barred, the factory occupied, and the manager locked up. Two coachloads of strikers set off immediately for the Renault plant at Flins in the Seine Valley to bring them out as well—the red flag was hoisted at 2 P.M.—and then on to the great Renault bastion in the Paris suburb of Boulogne-Billancourt, the parent and pacemaker of the whole state-owned car industry.

In the meantime, ever since the first spontaneous and disquieting outbreak at Nantes, the phone had been ringing in the Paris headquarters of France's two great trade union federations, the Communist-led CGT, and its Social Democratic rival, the CFDT. The union bosses were caught off guard by this extraordinarily militant phenomenon. What was the base up to? To forestall any further surprises, CGT headquarters acted swiftly. On Wednesday night it sent a hard-core commando to close down the Billancourt works and occupy the factory where 60 percent of the 25,000 workers are CGT loyalists. Four thousand men spent that night in the factory, sleeping on stretchers filched from the first-aid posts, or on bundles of rags, or on inflatable rubber mattresses, relics of last summer's holiday, which their wives had brought to the works with packages of sandwiches and bottles of wine. Within forty-eight hours, spreading with extraordinary speed, the strike and occupy movement paralyzed French industry across the country. Was this the concentrated action of fully mobilized unions? Or was it a semi-spontaneous process, springing from a decade of unsatisfied grievances and triggered in some mysterious way by the students' example and the police repression?

In those first few days of the strike no one in France was quite certain what was happening. Attention was, if anything, focused on the more spectacular developments on the student front—on the libertarian experiment being played out at the Sorbonne and, it soon appeared, in every other faculty in France. The union high commands did not know what to make of it and met that week in anxious sessions to try and see what the future might hold. Neither the CGT nor the CFDT could fail to be struck by the government's climb-down in the face of student violence and particularly by the way the student leaders had forced the government to release their imprisoned comrades. The government had also bowed to the twenty-four-hour general strike of May 13, even though it had been called without the statutory five-day warning. These were signs of weakness that could surely be exploited. It was here that the two most powerful union federations in France parted company. The Communist bosses of the CGT were obsessed by the threat on their flank, represented by activist *groupuscules* such as the Trotskyist JCR and the pro-Chinese UJC(M-L). These were doctrinal enemies that could be given no quarter. They threatened to outflank the party on its left and weaken its control over the working class. These considerations lie at the root of the CGT's attitude in the first week of the strike. It spared no effort to separate the workers from the students, issuing orders to its branch officials that no students were to be allowed inside factories under their control. It did not like the nature of the strike or its spontaneous genesis, and yet it was driven to take the leadership of it, to deny it to the uncontrolled "leftists." CGT tactics, therefore, were to cold-shoulder the student revolutionaries and to advance on behalf of the working class purely economic claims. It wanted for its members a bigger share of the capitalist cake, not, it would appear, the change or overthrow of the capitalist system.

The CFDT, in contrast, hastened to declare its sympathy

for the student movement. Several CFDT leaders went to the Sorbonne shortly after its occupation to listen to the furious debates and ponder their meaning. "The students not only are concerned with material considerations," the CFDT declared, "but seek to pose a fundamental challenge to the rigid and stifling class structure of a society in which they can assume no responsibility. The students' struggle to democratize the universities is of the same nature as the workers' struggle to democratize the factories. . . ."

The essential difference then between the two unions was this: The CGT saw the crisis as nothing but the work of "leftist adventurists"; the CFDT, free from the bonds of Communist dogma, was more penetrating. It sensed that more and more young people found French society, as at present organized, intolerable. One of the CFDT's ablest leaders, Albert Détraz, put it this way: "It is not an accident that black flags now challenge the monopoly of red flags in street demonstrations. There is here the rebirth of an ideal of liberty. It is a timely reminder to some political and union leaders that a society without real democracy is a barracks."

Thursday, May 16, was for M. Pompidou a turning point of the mounting crisis, and for a moment in those tense hours he must have doubted whether his policy of appeasing the students had been wise. The government that day faced two horrifying dangers. The first was that after triumphantly invading the Odéon Theater, which they had done on Wednesday, the student rabble army might attack and seize other government property. There was talk of its marching on the radio station. The second danger was that the powerful Communist-led CGT might swallow its doubts about the student leaders and throw its immense weight behind them. An astounding scene took place at the Ministry of the Interior. Christian Fouchet, the minister, called in his aides to seek their advice on which public buildings should be defended by force, if the students attacked. Was

the Théâtre Récamier in this class, or the French Academy?
No one felt strongly about them, but the concensus was that
foreign opinion would be alarmed if the Comédie Française
were to fall. It takes a revolution to show up the irrelevance
of a country's ancient monuments.

M. Pompidou held a council of war—one of several that
week with his security and political advisers—and decided
to address the nation on Thursday night. It was essential, he
felt, to split the handful of revolutionary student leaders
from their mass following and, still more vital, to keep
workers and students apart. He considered that the wisest
course was to show the public what the revolutionaries were
really like. At eight thirty that evening—an hour before the
Premier was due to speak—Daniel Cohn-Bendit, Jacques
Sauvageot, and Alain Geismar were put on television
opposite three seasoned journalists. But Pompidou's ploy
failed. The youngsters made mincemeat of the somewhat
sheepish publicists, who, with the student revolt still on a
rising curve, were reluctant to seem too hostile to it. But
when his time came to speak, M. Pompidou pledged, in
the most somber tones, that the government would defend
the republic. "Students," he pleaded, "do not follow the
agitators. . . . Listen to the voice of reason. . . . Citizens, it
is up to you to demonstrate . . . that you refuse anarchy.
The government will do its duty. It is asking you for your
help." He seemed that night a very lonely man. Jokes
circulated in Paris about De Gaulle heading a "government
in exile" in Rumania. But pleasantries apart, the specter
of real and probably bloody revolution hung somberly over
France.

After the broadcast the Premier and the President talked
at length on the telephone between Paris and Bucharest.
General de Gaulle decided to cut short his visit to Rumania
by the best part of a day and return to Paris on Saturday,
May 18. Orders went out for the call up of reservists for
the *gendarmerie*. But even as De Gaulle and Pompidou

spoke, this first dangerous corner for the government had already been turned. The French Communist Party in a statement issued late on Thursday night denounced the proposed march on the radio station as a "provocation." At midnight the students, feeling isolated, called it off. That same Thursday night a group of them, about 1,000 strong, marched from the Sorbonne to the great Renault works on the Seine at Boulogne-Billancourt, which had struck that afternoon. They carried a banner which said, "This flag of struggle will pass to the workers from our fragile hands." The workers thanked them courteously but would not let them in the factory, so the students marched around the works singing the "Internationale." Small groups of students and workers formed here and there in the street, and talk continued late into the night. "To begin with," one student said later, "we chose rather simple words and spoke slowly as if to foreigners. But we found they spoke the same language as we did." The Communist union bosses would have none of such fraternization. "Who is Cohn-Bendit?" CGT Secretary-General Georges Séguy said, with the dismissive mock ignorance of a Supreme Court judge seeking to identify Elizabeth Taylor. The fateful wedding of workers and students was not yet to be, and for the moment the republic was reasonably safe.

On May 14, 200 men were on strike; on May 19, 2,000,000; on May 22, more than 9,000,000. The paralysis spread with incredible speed and spontaneity. At no time did a general strike order go out from the Paris headquarters of the union federations, and yet all over the country a calm, irresistible wave of working-class power engulfed the commanding heights of the French economy. In thousands of plants the workers not only struck but also locked themselves in with their silent machines, turning the factories into fortified camps.

The revolutionary students cannot claim the credit for

this vast resolute stoppage, but they undoubtedly had something to do with it. The analogy with the student occupations was too blatant. The student protest was steeped in the vocabulary of the workers' struggle and in the ideal of workers' brotherhood. From May 3 onward the student leaders called persistently for a workers' revolt. It was as if they were trying to revive in the proletariat forgotten traditions of militancy. Who can tell what emotions they awakened? Old workers with memories of past struggles may have been stirred by the combativeness of these young intellectuals, and young workers, not yet reconciled to the view that life is just the pay envelope, may have thrilled in turn to the cry from the Sorbonne. In every university town across France, workers and students met and fraternized in the streets. These things cannot be proved, but it is hard to believe that the solidarity young people feel for one another did not play a role or that the workers were not impressed by the effectiveness of direct action as a weapon in the students' hands. Would it have happened had the workers not seen the government reel back from the clash at the barricades? Would it have happened if the great demonstration of May 13 had not reminded the strikers of their numbers and their power? One thing is certain: The great well-oiled union apparatus of the CGT, as well as its less powerful sisters, the CFDT and *Force Ouvrière,* did its best to channel and control the movement but did not provide the fuel.

The question is: What did? The fighting contribution of the students would have raised no echo in the working class had it not found there a mass of frustrations. First was the crude fact that minimum wages in France were scandalously low and that, in the ten years of Gaullist rule, the gap between workers' incomes and those of the managerial class had widened. This prosperity, of which they had little part, could no longer be hidden from the workers; it was rammed down their throats by television and by increasingly pervasive advertising vaunting the *dolce vita* of a consumer society. Before the May-June wage settlements, a quarter of all French wage earners earned less than 550 francs a month (about $110) and a third earned less than 720 francs (about $144); about 1,500,000 wage earners on the very bottom of the scale—unskilled industrial workers and agricultural laborers—made little more than 400 francs a month (about $80). For much of this underprivileged population, hourly rates had fallen well behind those of France's Common Market partners (except Italy), and only heavy overtime allowed many workers to climb above subsistence level. These abysmal figures are only part of the picture. By May, 1968, French unemployment had soared to more than 500,000, hitting not only depressed areas, as in many other industrial countries caught in a process of transformation, but particularly the young. In Burgundy, for instance, home of the Socialist leader François Mitterrand, 29 percent of young people under twenty-five were unemployed.

This was the raw material of the great restlessness which simmered just below the surface of the French working class and which, long before the May crisis, broke out in sporadic acts of industrial violence. Riot police and young workers fought fiercely at Caen and at Le Mans in the autumn of 1967, and that same year Rhodiacéta's synthetic fibers complex was paralyzed by a long, tough strike. Here were precursors of a revolt at the base which unions, employers and government failed to diagnose. More and more workers—and particularly the under-thirties who in May were the motor of the working class—were bitterly dissatisfied with what their unions had done for them. They had become skeptical of the whole tradition of negotiating cap in hand and of the meaningless demonstrations of workers' solidarity, such as the march through Paris from the Bastille to the Place de la République, more a picnic than a show of proletarian militancy. The notion that if it were to bring the employers to the negotiating table, it must act from strength, was gaining among the working class. This was the profound meaning of the factory occupations and the frequent locking up of managers; it was direct action on the factory floor, a gun at the boss' head, a resort to naked strength so often symbolized by the macabre sight of straw-filled dummies, labeled CAPITALISM, dangling from makeshift gallows in the factory yard.

The situation inside many French factories is positively medieval by British or American standards. Companies like Michelin used to boast that they had talked to strikers only three times in thirty years. Peugeot in June called in the riot police to clear its factories, and in the skirmishes, two men were killed. Citroën has a reputation among workers for being more like a penitentiary than a factory. Union rights are negligible. Men of different nationalities—Algerians, Yugoslavs, Spaniards—are often placed side by side on the production line to cut out talking. One-third of the workers in Citroën's Paris plants are immigrants housed in company hostels. Thousands more of these foreign workers—particularly Spanish and Portuguese—are employed in big French engineering plants. Their work permits can be withdrawn by the police under pressure from the companies. This is an important brake on union militancy. Nothing could match the joy and sense of liberation with which the Citroën plants were occupied.

Not all companies are as strict as Citroën, but most are traditionally secretive and paternalistic. Their published accounts are virtually meaningless. Workers are told little of management plans, production targets, or possible short-time working. This secrecy extends to lower managerial levels; this may be one reason why the great majority of skilled men and supervisory grades strongly backed the May-June strike.

These nineteenth-century conditions have survived in

France in part because French unions have not been able to put up much of a fight since the Second World War. The explanation is complex, but it has something to do with the fact that the Communist-led CGT has shied away from anything that might seem like treasonable collaboration with the capitalist enemy. The CGT focused its attention on wage levels, disdaining involvement in corporate affairs, a guaranteed working week, a minimum monthly wage—let alone the formation of works councils. To show an interest in them would be an acknowledgment that private capitalism was here to stay. This CGT attitude suited a large number of older French workers who still had roots in the land. They wished to have nothing to do with French industrial capitalism except to draw money from it.

But a new generation that finds inadequate this view of a union's role is growing up. It believes workers' representatives should be involved in decision making at plant level; it is deeply concerned with the recognition of union rights and the spread of information from the manager's office downward. These ideas have found a champion in the CFDT, which, although now independent of the Catholic Church, remains permeated with the radical philosophy of French left-wing Catholicism. Here is at least one source for the view, heard constantly among workers during May, that work is more than money and that human dignity is as valid a union claim as a bigger pay envelope.

To summarize what is a complex and constantly moving subject, the CGT is wage-oriented, while the CFDT seeks profound reforms at the factory level to give the workers a direct share in management. What was striking about the May crisis is that it saw the emergence of yet a third trend on the French labor scene, as hostile to the CFDT as to the CGT. The trend was frankly revolutionary; its ambition to overthrow capitalism led it first to attempt to undermine the Communist-led CGT monolith, which it saw as an unwitting pillar of the bourgeois state.

These were the pressures to which George Séguy, the neat, plumpish forty-one-year-old secretary-general of the CGT, was subject in May. A cool-headed organization man and a lifelong Communist, he has been a member of the party's Central Committee from the age of twenty-seven. For a few days last May he seemed to hold the destiny of France in his hands. A revolutionary minority at the base of his federation, inspired and encouraged by the students, sought to stampede him into insurrectionary action. He was racked by the fear of being bypassed by the extreme left, of being left behind by his rank and file, of missing the chance —perhaps the chance of a lifetime—of making a bid for power on a national level. The revolutionaries applied a sharp stick to the rump of the lumbering CGT elephant, but the beast would not be moved. The French Communist Party was not persuaded that a truly revolutionary situation existed—and President de Gaulle is still on his throne.

General de Gaulle returned home from Rumania on Saturday, May 18, to find France idle and the opposition baying for the government to go. In the five days he had been out of the country the Great Strike had spread beyond all expectations and was still spreading. Millions of workers had downed tools. All air and rail traffic was at a standstill. Postal deliveries had dried up. There was no public transportation in Paris, Nice, Marseilles, and a string of provincial towns. Banks were running out of cash and having to ration their customers. The threat from the students seemed small compared to the forces now ranged against the government. But the President was in a combative mood. The first minister he called to the Élysée on Sunday morning, the morrow of his arrival, was Pierre Messmer, Minister of the Armies. It was rumored that De Gaulle's instinct was to speak out strongly and bring the country to order. He had found it profoundly humiliating to be out of the country, preaching his gospel of national independence to the Rumanians, while France was in anarchy.

But the patient rocklike Pompidou persuaded him that silence was the best policy. It had been decided that the President would address the nation on Friday, May 24, a week after his return. Dignity now demanded that this schedule should be respected. One tart, sneering phrase leaked out from the Élysée: "Reform, yes. Bed messing, no!"* This was the general's appraisal of the enemy's order of battle. To those who saw only the surface of events, De Gaulle's remark seemed dangerous and provocative. But the government strategists were not dismayed. They knew the government would survive the motion of censure tabled by the opposition and due to be voted on Wednesday, May 22. They noted with relief the growing estrangement between the Communist Party and the revolutionary students; it was evident that Waldeck Rochet, his Central Committee, and the CGT would not easily allow themselves to be stampeded into insurrection. It was also clear for everyone to see that the marriage between the Communists and M. Mitterrand's Socialists—the only combination which could provide a credible alternative to M. Pompidou's government—was far from consummated. The Communists were pressing M. Mitterrand to put his signature to a common program of government—that is to say, a contract guaranteeing the Communists a share of power if the left were to take over. But M. Mitterrand and his Socialist federation were shifty; they called only for the resignation of the government and general elections. In the headlong course of events Mitterrand wanted his hands untied. Finally, the CGT and CFDT were having trouble concerning their joint strike action and agreeing on the claims they wanted satisfied. Here, too, the government hoped to divide and go on

* *La réforme, oui. Le chienlit, non.*

ruling. Concerned at this disarray on the left, Pierre Mendès-France, the lonely prophet of French politics, stepped for the first time into the ring with a short condemnatory statement: "There is only one service," he declared, "which the government can now render the country: It can withdraw. . . ."

General de Gaulle and his Prime Minister now judged the moment ripe to seize the initiative. The plan devised was two-pronged: first, to recognize by a gesture the spectacular and dramatic nature of the stoppage which was paralyzing the country, by proposing an equally spectacular settlement on the lines of the Matignon agreements of 1936. These had been round-table talks between government, employers, and unions which had brought the working class unprecedented benefits. The suggestion of a 1968 Matignon was all the more effective since the bosses of French industry had always insisted on piecemeal negotiations at the lowest possible level—the factory. Few of France's big firms ever consented to companywide, let alone industrywide, wage talks. It was felt that to propose nationwide discussions at the highest level would take the fight out of the unions while at the same time bringing the almost equally troublesome *patronat* to heel. Although authoritarian and steeped in conservative tradition, General de Gaulle has no love for unregenerate French capitalism.

The second line of the government's counterattack was the magic weapon of the word "participation," which, it was decided, General de Gaulle would launch on the public in his speech on Friday. He would call on all French citizens to pronounce on his plan by referendum. Not only was the referendum a proved expedient—it had served the regime well on four occasions—but, it was thought, the offer of participation, nebulous and undefined as it was, would satisfy the longings of millions for a greater say in the running of their own affairs which was the true mean-

ing of the strike. There was a hint in participation of profit
sharing, of comanagement, of stern and haughty bosses un-
bending to their subordinates—there was something in it
for everybody.

By Wednesday, May 22, these plans were maturing
nicely. The government romped through the formality of
the censure debate with eleven votes to spare, two Gaullists
providing, however, a touch of drama—just enough to
allow one to suppose the fight was for real. Both were men
with national reputations on the left of their party, and
both defected from the Gaullist ranks. René Capitant resigned his parliamentary mandate to avoid having to vote
against the government. Edgard Pisani voted against and
then resigned. Capitant's was considered the more honor-
able course. He is a friend and a great admirer of General
de Gaulle, and his gesture caused a little flutter. But the
overall outcome was not in doubt, and the government—
at least in its own estimation—emerged stronger from the
ordeal.

That same day Daniel Cohn-Bendit, leader of the March
22 Movement, was declared "undesirable in France." The
Ministry of the Interior announced that Cohn-Bendit, then
between Berlin and Amsterdam, would not be allowed entry
at any French frontier post. Strong forces of riot police
marched to the heart of the Latin Quarter, taking up osten-
tatious positions in the square opposite the Sorbonne after
an absence of three days. All these were pointers to the
government's growing, if misguided, confidence.

There was something a little unreal about these neat
political calculations in the midst of the great hush. Industrial noise died in France as everything seemed to head for
a state of nature. The complex interdependent networks
of a modern society collapsed, to be replaced by what
seemed a pattern of dancing and liberated atoms. Men fell

back on themselves, in their homes or their places of work. It could have been a bonus vacation, a deliciously prolonged day off, untroubled by pangs of conscience or a nagging wife. Indeed, wives and children joined the strikers on Sundays, turning the factory yards into gay fairgrounds. It was as if the working class had opted out of the political struggle. And yet, on another view, this casual idleness, this proprietory lolling about the works, were the essence of revolution. Never had workers talked so much, thrashed out so many puzzles, got to know one another so well, or so meticulously explored those clean carpeted rooms where the managers used to rule. No closet door was left unopened.

The strike reached its peak on May 22, leaving untouched no corner of the country. At Berliet, the great commercial vehicle manufacturers in Lyons, the workers, in a giant game of Scrabble, rearranged the letters on the front of the factory to spell *liberté*. The Paris headquarters of the French employers' federation—a club for the top bosses if ever there was one—was occupied for two hours by commandos of insurgent engineers. The merchant navy was out, and the undertakers, and some big Paris hotels. Department stores put up the shutters on all their gay windows, and hundreds of town halls were closed. Even the august Bank of France and the Finance Ministry and the atomic plant at Marcoule were not spared. Even the weather forecasters struck. It was extraordinarily and delightfully quiet. Gasoline was running short, but there was no real panic; some anxious housewives stripped clean their local grocery shops, but their example was not widely followed. Paris was filthy, strewn with garbage and political tracts. But the predominant mood was not alarm, but joy and liberation. With the collapse of public transportation, people rediscovered their legs. Friendships sprang up in the great march along the sidewalks. Shyness and modesty and snobbery were swept away, as everyone turned hitch-hiker. The atmosphere was as gaily libertine as on a war-time holiday, and the spring air was intoxicating. *Salut, camarade!*

11   Mini-Experiment in Revolution: Nantes, 1968

> We will claim nothing.
> We will ask for nothing.
> We will take.
> We will occupy.

TEXT FROM A SORBONNE WALL

FOR six remarkable days, from May 26 to May 31, 1968, the city of Nantes, at the head of the Loire Estuary in southern Brittany, was the seat of what amounted to an autonomous soviet. A Central Strike Committee—representing workers', peasants', and students' unions—set itself up in the town hall, becoming in effect the real local authority. The prefect, representing the central government in Paris, was left with no staff except a doorman and a small force of police which he dared not use.

Short-lived and chaotic though it was, this experiment in workers' power was nevertheless of considerable historical importance. In Nantes the strikers crossed the frontier from protest to revolution. There emerged embryonic institutions replacing those of the bourgeois state which were paralyzed by the strike. Here was an example of that *double pouvoir* for which the revolutionaries longed. But the example was not followed, and in Nantes it did not survive by more than a few hours General de Gaulle's tough May 30 speech. As we saw in the last chapter, the CGT was ferociously opposed to any such insurrection, while the mass of workers throughout the country wanted none of it. It is in any event doubtful whether industrial societies can tolerate the anarchy of such direct democracy. But it did happen in Nantes —that was no illusion. Its failure to spread was a source of bitter disappointment for the student leaders who, from the first occupation of the Sorbonne, called out to the workers to join them in revolution.

There were spectacular moments during the May crisis when the junction of students and workers appeared to take place, such as at the great demonstration of May 13 and at the mass meeting in the Charléty Stadium on May 27 (an account of which will be given in Chapter Fourteen). The brotherhood of youth was in the air, breaking down barriers of class and nationality. Groups of students marched to the factories in support of the strikers. In the Sorbonne (and later at the Institute of Psychology in the Rue Serpente) a Student-Worker Liaison Committee* tried to keep track of the many spontaneous contacts that sprang up. Workers from plants in the Paris area would come to the committee to seek student help—particularly in June, when the strike movement was under strain and cracking up. Boys and girls, members of the JCR, visited factories in twos and threes with all the dedication and humility of missionaries, in an attempt to start discussions, distribute tracts, and spread the word that the CGT was a fossilized bureaucracy in the service of the bourgeois state and that a new revolutionary leadership had to be created on the factory floor. Still more devoted were militants of the pro-Chinese UJC(M-L), whose philosophy of "Serving the People" led them to abandon their studies and sign on as laborers in workshops, the better to spread their revolutionary doctrines. These young people, whether Trotskyist or Maoist, were like guerrillas operating in enemy territory, gunned for by the powerful CGT union machine. They

* *Comité de Liaison Étudiant-Ouvrier* (CLEO).

were morally admirable but achieved little. Unlike their British and American equivalents, French unions cannot boast of a large, fully paid-up membership. They tend to enjoy the same sort of support as political parties: The workers know which union they want to follow but do not necessarily join it. But their small membership does not make them ineffective. They are tightly knit and strictly disciplined. To challenge the CGT, for instance, in a French factory is no picnic.

What the student revolutionaries hoped for was that the workers would move beyond the strike and occupy phase and actually encroach on the powers of the managers. They wanted to see workers' institutions set up at factory level, which would be the precursors of a workers' state. These ambitions were not satisfied in May; many other developments took place at the factory level, but not quite that. There was an explosion of talk in the long idle days of the strike, such as the workers had probably never known before. Strike committees across the country organized pickets and watchtowers and catering, as well as fun and games for the families on Sundays. In a score of factories, managers were locked up in their carpeted offices. In a handful of firms, committees sat down to draft schemes for more democratic management.* But there was no generalized assault on the power of the *patron*. Had there been, the reaction of the ruling class might well have been sharper.

At 3 P.M. on May 14, 1968, union representatives at Sud-Aviation's Bourguenais plant, near Nantes, decided to lock the manager in his office, where he was joined by some of the supervisory staff. The strikers placed a guard at his door. A loudspeaker was rigged up outside the office, to

* Supervisory grades at Sud-Aviation's plant at Suresnes drafted an ambitious scheme for the "democratic management" of the whole French aircraft and space industries. See Josée Doyere, in *Le Monde* (June 26, 1968).

blare out revolutionary songs "so that the boss could learn the 'Internationale' without ideological effort." * (The noise was so deafening that the guard pickets complained and ultimately the songs were switched off.) Watchtowers were built around the factory walls and manned by workers, who that night slept in packing cases. This plant, employing 2,800 workers, was the first to be occupied in France. It detonated the movement that spread so soon to the whole country.

Nantes has a long history of bloody-mindedness and poor labor relations. With its twin town of St.-Nazaire, it was rebuilt after the devastation of war on a declining industry—shipbuilding. A hard-core Communist faction grew up in the local labor movement, able to bring the strikers out at a moment's notice. This naturally discouraged new industries from moving into the area. Renault, for instance, when planning a new plant, rejected the Loire Estuary and instead chose Flins in the Seine Valley. Sud-Aviation put up its plant there with great reluctance and has had nothing but trouble ever since. There was a lockout in 1957, when the works were occupied by police, followed by other lockouts in 1960 and 1962. Early in May, 1968, the CGT (800 members at Sud-Aviation), the CFDT (700), and FO (300) decided to call a strike when the management refused to consider claims for a shorter working week without a wage cut. This was the background to the locking up of the manager, M. Duvochel, on May 14. Soon the strikers got organized. They built shelters to sleep in; they played games to keep themselves amused; volunteers ran a canteen.

As at Nanterre, students at Nantes played a vital role in whipping up revolutionary sentiment. On May 7 students and teachers went on strike in sympathy with the university protest, which by that time was nationwide. When the wild-

* For details of the Nantes strike, see *Cahiers de Mai*, No. 1 (June 15, 1968).

cat strike broke out at Sud-Aviation on May 14, students rushed to the workers' support with money and with blankets taken from university hostels. They reinforced the strike pickets. Schoolchildren joined the movement and on May 11 took part in an assault on the Nantes Railway Station. The unions, cool at first to these offers of help, gradually warmed to the students and finally allowed UNEF and the FEN (*Fédération de l'Éducation Nationale*) to join the Central Strike Committee, which became the chief authority in the town on May 26. On it sat the three principal trade unions, two peasant unions—FNSEA and CNJA*—and the university unions.

The first task the committee assumed was the control of traffic entering and leaving the town. Already, on May 24, striking transport workers had erected roadblocks on the four principal approach roads to Nantes, which they manned with the help of schoolchildren and university students. When the Central Strike Committee was set up on May 26, it started issuing gasoline coupons, as well as travel permits, to truck drivers carrying essential supplies for the strikers or for the farms in the surrounding areas. (The system was rather chaotic; one of the largest factory owners in Nantes applied for a permit—and got it.) The local police did not dare disperse their forces in order to attack the roadblocks, while the town halls of the region winked at the new arrangements. For several days the city was thus cut off from the outside world and under the workers' control.

A parallel, equally revolutionary development was taking place inside the city, particularly in the working-class quarter of Les Batignolles, where, from May 24 onward, the wives of striking workers decided to take in hand food deliveries to local shops. They set up a *comité de quartier*, and their example was soon followed in other working-class

* *Fédération Nationale des Syndicats d'Exploitants Agricoles* and *Centre National des Jeunes Agriculteurs.*

districts. These district committees made contact with the Central Strike Committee, which, on May 29, opened six retail trade outlets in schools. The peasant unions had in the meantime called on their members to cooperate in feeding the strikers. Teams of workers and students went out to help the farmers pick the new potatoes. By cutting out middlemen, the new revolutionary authorities slashed retail prices: A liter of milk fell from 80 to 50 centimes; a kilo of potatoes from 70 to 12 centimes, and of carrots from 80 to 50 centimes. The big grocery stores were forced to close. Some small shops were allowed to open, but trade union officials checked the prices every morning. The unions helped the poorer families of strikers by distributing food chits: one franc's worth of milk for children under three years old and, for children over three, 500 grams of bread and one franc's worth of other food. Teachers set up nurseries for strikers' children.

Workers and peasants, so often at loggerheads, started working together. Power workers made sure there was no break in the electric current for the milking machines; normal deliveries to farms of animal feed and gasoline were maintained. Peasants came to march the streets of Nantes side by side with workers and students. Thirty-two years earlier, in 1936, more than 500,000 peasants, mostly employed on great estates, had demonstrated in Nantes against the Popular Front. This was Chouan country— scene of the great royalist peasant revolts at the close of the eighteenth century. But times had changed. Last May the Place Royale was renamed the Place du Peuple.

Thus, for a few days, Nantes experienced the tentative beginnings of a popular government. It did not last, except as a burning memory in the strikers' minds. By May 31 the threat of a police assault became more worrying. The Whitsun weekend brought a slackening in militancy. By June 1 the Central Strike Committee decided to give up gasoline rationing because it was unpopular with motorists, and on the night of June 1–2 the roadblocks were taken down because it was feared that Paris would send armed convoys to the town. The seige was lifted; life returned to normal; the prefect recovered his powers. But Nantes had had its precious mini-revolution.

12 Abortive Settlement

ONE of the major victims of the May crisis was the close and confident relationship between President de Gaulle and Georges Pompidou, the cunning and affable *Auvergnat* who had served him as Prime Minister for six years. Alone among the men of the Fifth Republic, Pompidou had emerged as a political leader in his own right, with a skill and popularity second only to that of the general. The clash between the two men may be dated to the highly charged twenty days from the Night of the Barricades on May 10–11 to General de Gaulle's speech on May 30— three weeks in which the life of the Fifth Republic was at stake. Pompidou's contribution to final success was steady, powerful, unrelenting; De Gaulle's, intermittent, uneven, spectacular. On display were two fundamentally different political styles. The Prime Minister emerged with greater honor. From May 30 onward his banishment was only a matter of time.

Not until the Élysée archives are opened (or Bernard Tricot, the inscrutable secretary-general of the presidential palace, writes his memoirs) will it be known what passed between the two men in that agonizing period. But it may already be asserted that Pompidou's major headache in that period was to reconcile what he felt convinced was the right policy with the general's choleric and high-handed political instincts. The period falls neatly into two phases: the first, from Pompidou's return to France on the morrow of the Night of the Barricades to his weekend marathon talks with unions and employers on May 25–27, resulting in the abortive Grenelle agreements; the second—shorter, more intense, more dramatic—from May 27 to May 30. Few intimate relationships could survive such a storm.

Called by the President from the prosperous obscurity of the Banque Rothschild in 1962, Pompidou had in six years of power forged a political will as resolute as that of his master. But his appreciation of the crisis was subtler, more down-to-earth and realistic, untrammeled by the burden of incarnating France. As we have seen, his policy was to appease the students and isolate their revolutionary leaders, to keep the Communists on the right side of insurrection, and to bring the unions to the conference table in a grand settlement which would make of Pompidou the savior of the hour and the architect of a radical new deal. By Wednesday, May 22, this policy seemed well on the way to success. Cohn-Bendit had been banned from France, the Communists had condemned him, and the unions had accepted the invitation to talk. General de Gaulle then intervened to sabotage—that at least is how Pompidou must have seen it—this program: first by announcing that he would address the nation on Friday, May 24, and refusing to change this hard-and-fast plan to match the course of events. The whole of France waited in suspense for what he might have to say. As a result, two precious days were lost before talks with the unions could begin on Saturday. The violence which flared up in the interim undoubtedly contributed to the failure of the negotiations. De Gaulle's second intervention was, of course, the speech itself.

Awaited with such anxiety, it was a profoundly pathetic anticlimax. Neither the man nor his text measured up to the moment. If the revolt to which he was reacting meant anything, it represented a violent liberation of the French mind from official control. De Gaulle could think of nothing better than to seek a reconfirmation of his old sweeping powers. He proposed asking the nation by referendum for a "mandate of renewal." He threw in his notion of participation, but defined it only in such meaningless generalities as "adapting our economy . . . to national and international necessities" and more in the same vein. Shouts of astonished derision greeted his speech at its broadcast to young demonstrators in the streets. Suddenly, before everyone's eyes, he seemed a tired and bankrupt politician.

For the first time, political Paris started seriously to imagine a world without De Gaulle. *L'après-gaullisme* became of consuming interest. Even the most faithful Gaullists began to despair. It was tragically obvious that De Gaulle had not grasped the thirst for consultation and dialogue felt in every sector of French life. No one was ready to give him a blank check. It seemed that too much of a radical nature had to be done in France for the general, at seventy-seven, to be entrusted with its doing. His chances of a *oui* at the referendum, proposed for June 16, were counted as poor.

Who can doubt that Georges Pompidou shared the common opinion that De Gaulle had made the greatest blunder of his career? It is thought that he tried to persuade the general to hold, not a referendum—with its overtones of Bonapartism—but elections, as the country demanded. But the general was inflexible.

De Gaulle's referendum speech created throughout the country a climate of uncertainty about the future of the regime, which, it soon became clear, cut the ground from under the hard-fought Grenelle agreements. If the Élysée were soon to be vacant, who could take seriously breadand-butter discussions about the SMIG—*salaire minimum interprofessionel garanti*—the minimum wage rate? More immediately the proposed referendum, judged wholly inadequate by the opposition, added fuel to the wave of violence which had flared up once more in the Latin Quarter since the midweek announcement that Cohn-Bendit had been banned from France. On Wednesday a student crowd had marched on the heavily guarded National Assembly, crying, "We are all aliens!" And even young Arabs from Algeria were heard to shout, "We are all German Jews!" The night ended in skirmishes with the police, which on Thursday night turned into more serious fighting, bringing in its wake the usual toll of wounded and hundreds of arrests. Nearly a fortnight had passed since the Night of the Barricades, and the street guerrillas had had time to rest and bind their wounds. Their tactics were now more elaborate and more skilled. Slingshots appeared in the rebel ranks, and empty cars were sent careening with loose brakes into police phalanxes. It is perhaps worth remarking that no youngster in the Latin Quarter that week held Cohn-Bendit's nationality against him. De Gaulle's philosophy, proclaiming the nation-state the only meaningful dimension for international politics, was rejected by the young whose red and black flags pointed to a longing for other, more universal values.

Pompidou gnashed his teeth, but the damage was done. The round-table talks to which he had summoned the unions and the employers opened on Saturday, May 25, in the worst possible conditions. That morning Pompidou had had to give the police instructions to disperse any further street demonstrations "with the greatest energy." Fighting had raged in Paris, Lyons, and other cities on Friday night —fighting so savage that Pompidou himself described it as "an evident attempt to trigger the outbreak of a civil war." In Lyons a fifty-two-year-old police inspector was crushed to death by a runaway truck sent against a police barrier by the insurgents. In the Latin Quarter a young man of twenty-six was killed by a piece of flying shrapnel. It was the worst night of civil disturbances Paris had seen since the late thirties, worse even than the Night of the Barricades. Eight hundred people were taken into custody.

About 1,500 were wounded, and a great courtyard of the Sorbonne was turned into a field hospital. One lecture hall was marked SURGERY, another GAS CASES. Ambulances screamed back and forth through the ravaged streets till well after dawn on Saturday, when the Left Bank wakened to a scene of terrible desolation. Felled trees lay across the streets, with burned-out skeletons of cars and rotting and smoldering rubbish.

Skirmishing started around the Gare de Lyon when some 20,000 demonstrators, mobilized by UNEF, SNESup, and Cohn-Bendit's March 22 Movement, decided to march on the Hôtel de Ville, seat of Paris's municipal council. A CGT demonstration, called earlier that Friday, dispersed peacefully, but many young workers went on to join the students, whose blood was up. General de Gaulle's speech, which the great crowd paused to listen to, further inflamed them. Almost immediately there were clashes with the police. Then, on orders from their leaders, the demonstrators split up into small groups, forcing the police to scatter also. In this way one student column was able to attack, virtually unopposed, the Paris Bourse, to which it set fire with cries of "Burn down the temple of capitalism!" Gradually, other columns fought their way back across the river to the Latin Quarter, lighting fires in the streets, throwing up barricades, and pounding the police with missiles of all sorts. A police station and a movie house were sacked and scores of cars destroyed. The police made free use of their grenade throwers and brought up pressure hoses, but it did not seem an unequal battle. At 3 A.M., in a lull in the combat, the Minister of the Interior, Christian Fouchet, issued a communiqué in which he called on the city to "vomit out" the criminal underworld—in French, *la pègre*—whom he blamed for the fighting. *"Nous sommes tous la pègre,"* cried the students. Not many politicians strayed abroad that night. One exception was Pierre Mendès-France who wanted to see for himself what was happening in the Latin Quarter. He spoke for a few moments in a Sorbonne amphitheater and then toured the barricades before calling in at UNEF headquarters. "I've come as a witness," he said.

This third bloody Friday—after May 3 and May 11—hardened working-class sentiment at a disastrous moment for Pompidou's negotiations. Young workers at the demonstrations carried banners saying, "Power for the workers!"; "Power is in the street!"; "Don't give in, Séguy!"; *"Adieu, De Gaulle!"* From one week to the next the tone of the demonstrations had changed. Now they were more openly insurrectional. The students and the young workers made it clear that their object was to overthrow the government, and in this cause they battled all night. They were seeking to demonstrate that violence could be a short cut to the transformation of society. But the unions did not share these aims; their immediate objective was the economic betterment of their members. Far from overthrowing M. Pompidou, they came to parley with him. But under intense pressure from the leftist guerrillas, the Communist-led CGT was being driven step by step away from its cautious position in the middle of the road. This was the measure of the students' triumph: They had shifted the whole spectrum of French politics to the left and given people a taste for direct extra-parliamentary action. The terrible jinn had been let out of the bottle, and it would take a lot of tuneful piping to get him in again. M. Pompidou piped away manfully. He seemed the only pillar standing in the government. He was a whole Cabinet to himself: his own Labor Minister, Finance Minister, Education Minister, Information Minister. He spent days without sleep and yet faced the television cameras. He smoked forty or fifty cigarettes a day, and yet his voice remained grave and clear. He seemed to govern, and De Gaulle to watch.

M. Pompidou's round-table talks with unions and em-

ployers* were held over the weekend of May 25–27 at the
Hôtel du Châtelet, seat of the Ministry of Social Affairs in
the Rue de Grenelle. The negotiations lasted a grueling
twenty-five hours, ending at 7:30 on Monday morning,
when M. Pompidou gave the results to the nation in a radio
talk at breakfasttime. For two days millions of workers,
idle in factories, followed the bargaining over their transistor radios. Scores of journalists camped at the ministry,
seizing on a phrase here or a smile there to plot the course
of the debates going on in the conference hall. From the
start M. Pompidou was the master of the conference room.
His technique, after the opening statements, was to take
each union leader separately into a side room and ask him
what *he* was really after. The CGT was disarmed when
Pompidou accepted almost without discussion an immediate and massive increase of more than one-third in the
SMIG, carrying this minimum rate up to three francs an
hour—an increase of no less than 35 percent. Minimum
wages in agriculture were pushed up by 56 percent. Some
shopgirls, who had been earning even less than the SMIG,
got a bumper 72 percent rise. The CFDT's claims for extensive union rights in factories were less easy to settle.
At a break in the talks, the CFDT boss, Eugène Descamps
—the man who had separated his federation from the Catholic Church and built it up into a rival to the CGT—declared in the lobbies: "The walls of this ministry are thick;
the clamor from the factories and the street does not seem
to penetrate the conference room." A much photographed

* Present on the union side were delegates from the *Confédération Générale du Travail* (CGT), *Confédération Française Démocratique du Travail* (CFDT), *Confédération Générale du Travail–
Force Ouvrière* (CGT-FO), *Confédération Française des Tra-
vailleurs Chrétiens* (CFTC), *Confédération Générale des Cadres*
(CGC), and the *Fédération de l'Education Nationale* (FEN). The
employers were represented by the *Conseil National du Patronat
Français* (CNPF) and by the *Confédération Nationale des Petites
et Moyennes Entreprises* (CNPME). The Prime Minister was
flanked by J.-M. Jeanneney (Minister of Social Affairs) and
J. Chirac (Secretary of State for Labor). National agricultural
organizations were represented by an observer.

and interviewed delegate was Benoît Frachon, the seventy-three-year-old president of the CGT, who thirty-two years earlier had been a signatory of the 1936 Matignon agreements.

All the men involved in the vast negotiation were deeply conscious of the need to reach an agreement—even if their motives differed. For M. Pompidou, his career seemed to stand or fall on a successful outcome. It was the logical conclusion of the policy of appeasement and conciliation, spiced with firmness, which he had pursued against great odds since his return from Afghanistan. For the union leaders, substantial concessions secured at the conference table would, they hoped, allow them to cut the ground from under the feet of the troublesome leftists. Both sides were aware that failure, in the current climate of violence, could tip France from a national crisis into a state of revolution with results unpredictable for everyone.

Finally, a draft agreement was hammered out, conferring what seemed unprecedented advantages, relating to wages, the working week, the age of retirement, family allowances, old people's allowances, union rights, and so on—the biggest benefits secured for the working class since the Liberation. The strikers were to get half their normal pay for the days of idleness. Weary but content, the union leaders smiled as they trooped out of the Hôtel du Châtelet on Monday morning. The base—the rank and file waiting by their machines—still had to give its agreement, but to the tired negotiators that morning, the worst seemed over. They were wrong. The real crisis was only just beginning.

13 The Adult Left and the Crisis

In the last week of May, 1968, one question dominated all others: Would De Gaulle survive? The issue of power was thus squarely posed: Would the regime retain control of the state, or would power pass to other hands? Even if every other aspect of the May crisis is the subject of fierce controversy, everyone—whether Gaullist or non-Gaullist, revolutionary or democrat—will surely agree that this question was wide open.

If the regime fell, who could succeed it? No one imagined that the tiny revolutionary minorities that had detonated the crisis could aspire to rule. They were guerrillas operating on the fringes of society, not contenders for the succession. They wanted to torpedo the bourgeois state, not inherit it. Cohn-Bendit was not going to preside over the first-floor Cabinet room in the Élysée Palace. The only possible successors were the official opposition on the left. Some combination of Communists and Socialists was the only credible alternative—and not all that credible—to Gaullism. The crisis, then, was as challenging a test for the adult left as it was for the regime. Ever since the crisis exploded in early May, the left had been the butt of much criticism. It had been accused not only of blindness and cowardice, but also of naked illegitimate ambition; not only of betraying the revolution, but also of plotting it; not only of not having gone far enough, but also of having gone too far. These accusations spring from a number of confu-

179

sions about the nature of the left in France, as well as about
the exact nature of the political crisis with which the country was confronted in May.

When the crisis came, it found the left divided and unready: divided, both because Communists and Socialists,
although embarked on a flirtation, were still far from
married, and because the Socialists themselves were one
of those families where the wife despises the husband and
the children despair of both; unready because, to put it
bluntly, neither Communists nor Socialists really expected
the question of the succession to be posed before 1971–72.
That was the target date to which they were placidly
cruising. The crisis caught them with their trousers down;
they had been too slow.

The Gaullist regime was seven years old before François
Mitterrand, a Socialist lawyer and Fourth Republic politi-
cian, joined forces with the Communist Party leader,
Waldeck Rochet, in an attempt to defeat it. The occasion
was the presidential election of December, 1965, in which
Mitterrand stood as the "sole candidate" of the whole left.*
This tactical alliance between Communism and Social
Democracy—two old and bitter rivals—proved highly
successful: Mitterrand forced De Gaulle into the humilia-
tion of a runoff election. Only on the second round did
De Gaulle secure a clear majority of 54.5 percent to Mitterrand's 45.4, other candidates having withdrawn in the
meantime. To have come so near to unseating the general
did the newly united left no end of good. It had repercussions inside each camp. It allowed Waldeck Rochet, for
instance, to bring to heel old hard liners on his Central
Committee who had opposed the alliance with Social
Democracy. It allowed Mitterrand, in turn, to push ahead
with his task of welding the many different "families" of
the non-Communist left into a coherent federation. The

* This alliance was foreshadowed by a Communist-SFIO agreement of January 5, 1965, in the municipal elections for the Seine
Department.

federation's principal constituents are the Radicals, the oldest political party in France but in steady decline since its peak under the Third Republic; the Convention of Republican Institutions, one of the newest political formations in France, grouping about sixty clubs and societies around the country; and, finally, Guy Mollet's SFIO (*Section Française de l'Internationale Ouvrière*), re-created as a Social Democratic Party by Léon Blum when the majority of French Socialists joined the Comintern and turned Communist at the Tours Congress in 1920. Mitterrand sought by negotiation and subtle pressure to weld these three groups into one. His chief supporters were the Young Turks of the convention, a group of young men with energy and progressive ideals. His main obstacle was the fossilized political apparatus of the SFIO, not anxious to lose its identity and power to a wider grouping.

The relative success of the combined left at the December, 1965, presidential election encouraged the CPF and the federation to move still closer together. At the March, 1967, general elections they agreed on a tactical alliance which was pragmatic and nondoctrinal. It was limited to what the French call *désistement*—a mechanism set in train between the first and second rounds of legislative elections. This is the process whereby a candidate steps down in favor of a lesser enemy, better placed than he himself, in order to defeat an irreconcilable opponent of both. The arrangement between the CPF and the federation was that they should step down in favor of each other in order to defeat the Gaullists. In the event, the CPF and its Socialist ally won 194 seats, eating into the Gaullist majority, which fell from 233 to 200 (or from 268 to 244, if Valéry Giscard d'Estaing's Independent Republicans are counted with the Gaullists). These results were so good that there seemed a real chance of the combined left's winning outright next time.

This drove the two partners to move beyond a purely

tactical entente and to explore the possibility of drafting a common program. They realized that the electorate would want to know whether they were sufficiently agreed on fundamentals to be able to rule together. After extensive debate, a common platform was presented to the public on February 23, 1968, setting out frankly the areas of agreement and disagreement. It was not yet a common program of government, but it was a move toward it.

For all its candor, the document did not however reflect the real state of relations between the two parties, which were still far from surmounting their deep-seated suspicion of each other. The crux of the matter was this: The Communists feared that M. Mitterrand would use their votes to carry him to the Élysée, only to turn against them and join forces with the center when he came to rule. The federation feared that if it entered a government with the Communists, it would be eaten alive on the 1948 Czechoslovak model. It became, in fact, a cardinal but unvoiced principle of Mitterrand's strategy that he would not consider entering a governing partnership with the Communists, unless his federation were strong enough to dominate it. He knew he still had a long way to go: In 1967 the federation polled 4,200,000 votes against the Communists' 5,000,000 (although the hazard of parliamentary representation gave the federation 121 deputies against only 73 for the Communists). Everyone knew the Communists were the stronger. Moreover, Waldeck Rochet's Central Committee also controlled the CGT, the most powerful trade union federation in France.

From then on, therefore, Mitterrand consistently avoided giving the Communists cast-iron guarantees of a share in any future government he might form if they were to win an election together. This was the ambiguity of his position; he strove to offer the public a credible left opposition to De Gaulle and yet did not dare bind himself irrevocably to the Communists, for fear of scaring off non-Communist voters who knew the federation was too weak to hold the Communists in check.

This was the—not wholly satisfactory—point which the Communist-Socialist *rapprochement* had reached on the eve of the May crisis. The milestones to unity were the December, 1965, presidential election, the March, 1967, general elections, and the common platform of February, 1968. But as the crisis was to demonstrate, unity was still a good way off.

The overriding aim of the French Communist Party in the last three years had been to emerge from the political wilderness in which it has languished since 1947 and to become acceptable as a participant in government. In spite of its large working-class vote, the party knows that it cannot realistically hope to muster a governing majority on its own. Its road to power within the parliamentary system must lie therefore in an alliance with the non-Communist left. Hence its *rapprochement* with Mitterrand's federation.

The French Communist Party has been much maligned. De Gaulle can win an election by scaring the electorate with the specter of a Communist revolution, but the truth is that the Communist Party has not been a revolutionary movement since the Second World War. This is partly because it was from its birth in 1920 a mass party, not an avant-garde splinter group like other European Communist parties. At the Tours Congress of December, 1920, four-fifths of the SFIO decided to join the Comintern, one-fifth only following Léon Blum. The Communist Party was thus the direct heir of pre-First World War French Socialism and had a broad base to build from. It did not have to create a new organization from scratch. Faithful to Soviet requirements, it was, however, a genuinely revolutionary party in the twenties and early thirties, backing Léon Blum's Popular Front government in 1936 only as a temporary tactic.

Thrown back into clandestinity by the Nazi-Soviet pact of August, 1939, the CPF staged a triumphant and patriotic comeback in the Resistance after Russia entered the war in June, 1941. This was its finest hour; its militants demonstrated in action their capacity for sacrifice and the effectiveness of their cell-like organization. Their reward came at the Liberation, with 26 percent of the vote in the October, 1945, elections and four key ministries in General de Gaulle's government. But they were finally excluded from power a year and seven months later when Paul Ramadier dropped them from his government in May, 1947, and they have not tasted power since. In that short spell, twenty-one years ago, the CPF became part of the governing system and has retained a profound nostalgia for it. This is not a revolutionary instinct. Moreover, the large Communist electorate, which gives the party credit for the great social reforms of 1936 and 1945–46, is itself profoundly reformist, not revolutionary. The party has, in fact, been made in the image of its members, who are firmly integrated into society, no longer its alienated underdogs.

Such was the CPF on the eve of the May crisis: longing for respectability; committed to an alliance with the federation as the only path toward the power it longed for; supported by an industrial working class, which in its immense majority wanted consumer goods, not revolution. It should be added that the party's leadership was no longer in its first youth, that none were men of outstanding political gifts, and—last but not least—that the Soviet Union, to which the party has remained undeviatingly faithful throughout its career, has plumped firmly for peaceful coexistence. The last thing the Kremlin wants is a revolution in France which would deprive Russia of the considerable support it derives from General de Gaulle's foreign policy.

This brief excursion into history has one aim only: to illumine the behavior of the left during the May crisis. The point to recall is that both Communists and Socialists were committed, severally and together, to lines of policy clearly laid down, which we have sketched in above. Critics of the left's conduct during the crisis often overlook this considerable background. The agonizing question the Communist Party faced in May, 1968, was whether a situation so novel had arisen as to justify the overthrow and abandonment of policies dictated by history and by its own profound nature. The party pondered the matter in the secrecy of its Politburo and decided that it had not.

How then did the Communist Party react to the crisis? The first point to make is that it was taken by surprise—like everyone else. Reasons for discontent among students and workers were clear for all to see, but no one in France predicted the May explosion. No one was prepared for it. But whereas some, particularly the government, improvised —seizing on one expedient after another, switching policy in midstream, surrendering to panic—the Communist Party's reaction was at least ruthlessly consistent with the course it had been following before the crisis. The Politburo met daily and, at every stage of the unfolding drama, asked itself the question we have suggested above: "Does our policy still hold?" Each time—with the important exceptions we shall mention in due course—the Communist leaders stood firm. "We didn't lose our heads," said Waldeck Rochet with some justification after the storm had passed, when he reported to his Central Committee on July 8, 1968.

Part of the party's agony during the crisis was that it had to fight on two fronts, not only against the Gaullist regime, but against political guerrillas—Trotskyists, Maoists, Guevarists, and anarchists—on its left flank. Ever since the Sino-Soviet dispute began, the French Communist Party, like other Soviet-oriented Communist parties around the world, has been vigorously fighting (and expelling) pro-Chinese elements. The originality of the French situation, as we tried to show in Chapter Two, was that a whole generation of radical-minded young people had escaped from the party's control and turned against it, embracing not only Maoist positions but more particularly Trotskyist ones. On the level of youth organizations, this change was reflected in the withering of the orthodox Communist UEC (*Union des Étudiants Communistes*) and the growing strength of the Trotskyist JCR and the pro-Chinese UJC(M-L). This was a battle the Communists had been waging since 1966. It was, therefore, no accident that from the moment Cohn-Bendit raised his unruly red head in Nanterre, the Communist Party tried to cut it off.

The most striking demonstration of this hostility came on May 3, when, in *L'Humanité,* Georges Marchais, number two in the French Communist Party, violently denounced the "German anarchist, Cohn-Bendit": "Such false revolutionaries must be energetically unmasked," he declared, "because, objectively, they serve the interests of Gaullist power and of the great capitalist monopolies." At this early stage of the crisis the CPF misread the disturbances at Nanterre as a Chinese-inspired attempt to sabotage the Vietnam peace talks due shortly to open in Paris. The party's loathing for the UJC(M-L) was then at its height; a week earlier a Communist deputy, Pierre Juquin, had been hounded from a Nanterre lecture hall by a pro-Chinese commando.

As the crisis developed, the party tried to walk a tightrope between support for the students in the face of police repression and hostility to their extremist leaders. On May 9 the CPF's principal tame intellectual, the poet Louis Aragon, was booed at an open-air meeting on the Boulevard St.-Michel. Cohn-Bendit, with his gift for the wounding shaft, called on the writer to explain to the assembled thousands why *L'Humanité* attacked the March 22 Movement, and why "if you are on the students' side, you don't join them in the street." The Night of the Barricades forced the

Communist-led CGT, in brief alliance with the student unions, to back the general strike and massive demonstration of May 13—the occasion which drew from Cohn-Bendit his now-famous jeer at the "Stalinist filth" in the rear of the procession, his phrase for the Communist Party leaders.

Up to this point the mutual insults between the CPF and the leftist *groupuscules* were no more than routine skirmishing, continuing the running battle of the previous two years. But when the Great Strike movement began on May 14, the threat to the party from the student extremists suddenly became graver. Leading Communists, like Roland Leroy, who had originally opposed Georges Marchais' rough treatment of Cohn-Bendit and his friends, now rallied to the tough line. It was all-out war against the "leftist adventurists." The party feared that the extremists would incite hotheaded young workers in the factories to carry the strike over the dangerous frontier from peaceful occupation to setting up some form of workers' power and that by prolonging the strike, they might sabotage agreements reached with the employers. These fears haunted the CPF and CGT leadership precisely because the strike had started spontaneously and threatened to escape from their control. They knew that any success for the young revolutionaries would tint the whole workers' movement with an insurrectional flavor which they considered fatal to the interests of the working class. Hence the "iron curtain," behind which the CGT protected the striking factories, and its strict instructions that students should not be allowed inside. It was not until May 18 that the CGT was reasonably sure it had the strike movement well in hand and that the CGT boss, Georges Séguy, was able to describe his union, with a touch of complacency, as *la grande force tranquille*.

The dispute—which still rages—between the Communist Party and the *groupuscules* can be summed up in the question: Was there, or was there not, a revolutionary situation in France in May, 1968? The student leaders, drunk with the conviction that Trotsky's theories were coming true before their eyes, were certain that revolution was within their grasp. The Communists were equally certain that this was a profound and dangerous error. It was no academic argument. There was much at stake, perhaps even the lives of countless workers and the future of the whole French labor movement, as well as of the Communist Party itself. It is hard to believe that the party was not right in refusing to be stampeded into insurrection. This was not 1789, or Russia in 1917, or even Germany after the defeat of 1918. The great mass of French workers and peasants wanted more bourgeois comforts, not a new social order; the country as a whole was prosperous; the army was well equipped and loyal to the regime; the ruling classes were not ready to capitulate. Power was not so easily to be had. To reach out for it—by illegal means—was to risk a bloody civil war, for which the workers were unenthusiastic and unprepared. This was the Communist Party's analysis. It has earned them the charge from their enemies on the left of being bastions of the Gaullist establishment—indeed, even of being in collusion with it.

It was precisely because there was so much at stake that the party detested the "leftists"—described by Waldeck Rochet in his July 8 report as the "most pressing danger"; it was for the same reason that the CGT, resolutely opposed to the use of the strike as a revolutionary weapon, hated the CFDT's claims for workers' control; it was on this same score that the party savagely criticized the left-Socialist splinter group, the *Parti Socialiste Unifié* (PSU), which had opened its arms to the revolutionary students. Finally, this was part of the explanation why the Communists were uneager to work with Mendès-France when, as we shall see, he was proposed as a leader for the left in the last week of May. Had he not befriended the student revolutionaries?

It was part of the Communist Party's misfortunes that

harassed as it was on its left by the guerrillas, it found no comfort on its right with its chosen partners, François Mitterrand's Federation of the Left. As the crisis moved toward its denouement, it urged the federation, in daily more pressing fashion, to agree with it on a common program of government. Almost every issue of *L'Humanité* carried such a request. But Mitterrand would not be tied; his federation was too weak for him to risk presenting himself to the public, bound hand and foot by contract to the Communists. The crisis had pointed up their relative strengths: The Communists, through their unions, could hold the country to ransom, while he had no troops. Some of Mitterand's Young Turks rushed to the Latin Quarter during the fighting on May 23 with the cry "Your Shadow Cabinet has arrived!"—only to be sent packing with hoots of derision. But M. Mitterrand could not overlook the new and vigorous left in the student body, at the base of the working-class movement, in the hundreds of action committees all over Paris—springing up outside and against the Communist Party. Mendès-France was looking in this direction. Should not he do also? Thus, at the peak of the crisis, the union of Communists and the federation, planned for so long, did not take place, and no credible alternative to Gaullist rule emerged. But we are anticipating the next chapter.

The Communist Party's line was clear. It had turned its back firmly on insurrection. For twenty years it had dreamed of emerging from the ghetto reserved for political pariahs. On the labor front it was ready to back the strike in favor of economic claims alone. On the political front its aim was to supplant the Gaullist regime, in alliance with the non-Communist left—but acting *strictly* "within the framework of republican legality." Pursuing this cautious, moderate, deeply reasoned policy in May put the party under great strain. It was like a man selling stale bread when there is cake on offer. It came in for abuse; it suffered some spectacular defections, like that of André

Barjonet, head of the CGT's Economics and Social Studies Center, who accused the CPF of having betrayed the 1968 revolution and left to join the PSU. It expelled some revolutionary hotheads like Jean-Pierre Vigier, a Cuban sympathizer and a leader of the *Comité Vietnam National*. In every cell and in every factory, men asked whether the party was not missing the chance of a lifetime. But Waldeck Rochet, Georges Séguy, and their associates did not budge. It was, the secretary-general later declared: "the greatest achievement of our party and its leadership."

One further point remains to be elucidated if the attitude of the left during the crisis is to be understood. The CPF and the federation, their reluctant partners, and M. Mendès-France, who entered the political battle in its final stages, all were against insurrection and violent revolution. For a decade they had attacked De Gaulle's regime on the grounds that it had sprung from a *coup d'état*. They were not ready to stoop to the same methods. But there is a difference between overthrowing a regime by revolution and simply forcing it to give way when it already shows every sign of internal disintegration. The left was not guilty of the first, but it certainly attempted the second. This was the slender basis of De Gaulle's skillful but wickedly unfair charge that the republic was threatened with a Communist conspiracy. The charge won De Gaulle the June, 1968, elections, but robbed him finally of any lingering pretension to speak for the whole of France. But how the drama was played out must wait for the next chapter.

14   The Dangerous Week

PRESIDENT Charles de Gaulle, ruler of France for ten years and maker of history since 1940, was very nearly overthrown on Wednesday, May 29, 1968. A handful of rowdy students in a suburban annex to the University of Paris launched a nationwide movement of revolt which, within a month, exposed the fragility of what had seemed the strongest and stablest regime in Europe. For a few days at the end of May, France was on the brink of the unknown.

When the crisis had passed, and in the complacency of the old order recovered, many denied that the ground had ever moved beneath their feet. Some said that De Gaulle was only feigning when he fled Paris on May 29; that this was a dramatic masterstroke, intended to lull his enemies into overconfidence and prepare his own triumphant return. Even the Communist Party, a leading contender for the succession, has since claimed with baffling dialectic that never for a moment was power vacant and that to suggest that the party made a bid for it was absurd. Thus, history gets overlaid with myth.

The truth is that for a little less than four days, from May 27 to May 30, the crumbling of the state laid bare a great emptiness at its center. Men glimpsed the prospect of a new, wholly different, political order, a new organization of society. This fundamental uncertainty about the immediate future bred the sort of fear men experience in battle.

It drove housewives to overstock their larders and farmers, in the distant countryside, to put up their shutters and oil their guns.

Like the last act of a historical romance, those four days brought all the actors crowding on the stage, untangling their stories, resolving at last the patterns of their lives and policies. Pierre Mendès-France moved from the wings into the spotlight, to act out the last few hours of a tragically wasted political career, waiting for a call to office, as richly deserved as De Gaulle's, but which never came. Army generals like Jacques Massu, forgotten since the Algerian War, suddenly emerged as essential forces behind the scenes. Daniel Cohn-Bendit, clown and demon-king, banned from the France he had turned upside down, returned one midnight to the Sorbonne to mock the tottering adult world. François Mitterrand, a passionate, thin-skinned hero cursed by the gods, spoke up for Social Democracy, a lost cause in an arena dominated by the big battalions of the right and the left. Georges Pompidou, a more favored sort of hero, was like a man watching his fortune melt away on the Stock Exchange, only to be reprieved from final ruin by the news that an uncle had left him a million dollars. General de Gaulle, haunted by the terrible indignity of being overthrown by the street, glimpsed the abyss. He had to fight for his place in the Élysée and for a happy ending to his unfinished memoirs. In that last week of May, reputations swelled and collapsed like inflatable toys.

Supporting the movements of the principal actors were crowd scenes of Chinese proportions, enacted out of doors in the great open spaces Haussmann gave Paris. These popular demonstrations punctuated the week, marking with blinding symbolism the rise and eclipse of contending forces. They were political acts in Cinemascope with the sound track turned up high. This was no revolution in a glass of water, as the French say, no narrow juggling of parliamentary arithmetic in the style of the Fourth Republic. It was a cataclysm which nearly brought down the Fifth Republic and ushered in the Sixth. It was a denouement not just of a disturbed month, but of a whole epoch of French politics, a final and unkind comment on a Gaullist decade.

Monday, May 27, 1968, opened one of the worst weeks in De Gaulle's career. So disheartened was he that two days later he was, on his own admission, tempted to retire. He compared* this moment of despairing doubt with other troughs in his life. The first was in September, 1940, only three months after his glorious June 18 speech to occupied France, when an Anglo-Free French naval force failed to wrest Dakar from Vichy; for the first time in his life De Gaulle witnessed Frenchmen firing on Frenchmen. The second, in March, 1942, followed what he took to be a British-inspired plot against him inside the Free French ranks. The third was in January, 1946, when, sickened by the factiousness of French political parties, he abandoned office and retired to Colombey-les-deux-Églises. A fourth and a fifth time were in 1954, when he cut away from the *Rassemblement du Peuple Français,* which he had created in 1947, but which had been a failure, and in December, 1965, when François Mitterrand slashed his majority in the first round of the presidential election.

May, 1968, was the sixth time that De Gaulle, a public figure to his marrow, felt the lifeblood of popular acclaim ebbing from him. On that Monday every element of his government's policy lay in ruins. The referendum which he had proposed on the previous Friday, May 24, had run into a raging storm of opposition, setting off violence in the streets and provoking the *Conseil d'État* to denounce it as unconstitutional. Most humiliating, his speech had been dismissed as the blathering of an old man. It was clear to every politician that the whole referendum idea was a blind

* In a television interview on June 7 with Michel Droit.

alley. De Gaulle had failed to check the course of the revolt
But his Prime Minister, Georges Pompidou, was doing no
better. His patient, steadfast policy of appeasing the stu
dents and negotiating with the unions had also collapsed
in a shambles. The students, increasingly under the contro
of extremist leaders, were openly insurrectional, calling fo
the overthrow of the government with which they refused
all dealings. They would not be satisfied when Pompidou
looking for a scapegoat, accepted the resignation of Alain
Peyrefitte, the Minister of Education, and took over the
ministry himself. But the greatest blow to Pompidou was
the brutal rejection by the strikers of the terms of the
Grenelle agreements, which the Prime Minister had so
laboriously negotiated with the unions and employers.

At dawn on May 27 Pompidou emerged from the con
ference room, exhausted but triumphant, and himself read
the terms of the agreements to the nation. The union bosses
—Georges Séguy of the CGT, Eugène Descamps of the
CFDT, and André Bergeron of the *Force Ouvriére*—smiled
and gave the thumbs-up sign as they left to carry the news
to their members. By midmorning their smiles had withered.
Angry shop stewards bawled their protests down the telephone from every corner of the country. The unthinkable
had happened: The rank and file turned down the agreements and disavowed their leaders, leaving them far out on
a limb in an uncomfortable posture of seeming collusion
with the employers and the government. Still more alarming, the embattled strikers, looking beyond mere economic
benefits, raised the cry for a "government of the people."
It seemed horribly clear that the spark of revolution, struck
by the student extremists, had found tinder on the shop
floor. Suddenly revolution seemed everywhere in the air,
feared or hoped for. For the first time, solid citizens, canny
politicians, and the students grasped that the movement
begun as a utopian dream had made a real dent in the
political spectrum.

Some commentators have suggested that the CGT secre-
ary-general, Georges Séguy, and the veteran union presi-
lent Benoît Frachon already knew the Grenelle agreements
were doomed when they left the conference hall. The impli-
cation is that they wanted them rejected by the rank and
ile in order to escalate the crisis and bring down the government. The evidence is tenuous. It includes reports that
Georges Séguy was a surprisingly pliant negotiator, yield-
ing to M. Pompidou more easily than Descamps. Another
piece of evidence is that Séguy was constantly on the telephone during the negotiations and must, therefore, have
been well informed about the attitudes of the union base.
The CGT is a monolith, a spider's web of cells under rigid
central control. No dissident voice is tolerated. Anyone
who moves out of line, however slightly, cannot hope to
get a union job, however lowly—even collecting dues on
the factory floor. With this structure in view, it is hard to
see how Séguy could have misread his union's mood. Yet a
third fragment of evidence is that Séguy and Frachon had
arranged to drive out to the Renault plant at Boulogne-
Billancourt, where 25,000 workers were waiting for them
in the vast shed, before they knew the final terms of the
Grenelle protocol.

Were the union leaders, therefore, just playacting as a
prelude to insurrection? The great weight of evidence suggests that this interpretation is false. The CGT leaders and
their colleagues on the Politburo of the Communist Party
were as eager as the government to end the strike and protect the workers from the virus of extremist ideas. They had
done all that was humanly possible to keep the strike within
the bounds of strictly economic claims. Revolution was not
on the Communist Party's program, nor had it been since
the early fifties, if not earlier. This was the legacy which
Georges Séguy and the Communist Party's secretary-general, Waldeck Rochet, inherited from Maurice Thorez. The
basic, if unavowed, premise of Thorez's thinking was that

Communist revolution was impossible in France so long as
Russian living standards remained lower than those of
Western Europe. Once the Soviet Union had caught up,
then Europe would slide naturally toward a form of reformist Communism. In the meantime, the party's role was
to retain control of the French working class and prevent
itself being outflanked on the left.

As we suggested in Chapter Twelve, the Grenelle protocol, as negotiated that weekend, was a landmark in French
social history in the same league as the Matignon agreements of 1936 and the social legislation which followed
the Liberation. Séguy and Frachon must have felt that
they had led their union safely through the breach blown
open by the students and had secured enormous benefits
for the working class. At the same time they hoped they
had silenced the impatient younger workers, who, with the
active encouragement of the Trotskyists, had set their faces
against the union leadership.

But that Monday morning at Renault, Séguy's speech
was met with boos and whistles. From the first catcall, he
was in full retreat. In spite of all the information which
had flowed to him in the conference room, he had underestimated the success of an active minority in giving a
political content to the strike. He was faced with a situation
comparable to but far more dangerous than the one he had
confronted on May 14-15, when the unofficial strike and
occupy movement first got under way. Then he was driven
to seize the leadership of the movement in order to control
it. Now he too had to underwrite the strikers' call for a
popular government. But it must be said, and repeated,
that the CGT, like its controlling body, the CPF, never
seriously considered insurrection. To lifelong Communists
like Séguy and Waldeck Rochet, brought up in the Thorez
tradition, insurrection was a temptation of the devil, which
could only discredit the working-class movement and lead
to its savage repression. Hence Séguy's strictures, if any-

hing still more violent than Rochet's, against "leftists, anarchists, Trotskyists, pro-Chinese, and other troublemakers whom it is essential we defeat."*

The CPF and the CGT were accused by President de Gaulle and his ministers of revolutionary ambitions. As we have seen, this was unjust. But their position rested on an ambiguity which laid them open to such accusations. They wanted De Gaulle to fall, they underwrote the slogan of a "Government of the People," but they did not want to incur the odium of resorting to violence and illegality. They wanted to come into their kingdom by the front door with all due honor, rather than by breaking in. Such legitimist and highly respectable ambitions are difficult to satisfy in times of crisis. If one admits to wanting power, one exposes oneself to the charge of planning to seize it.

This, then, was the unnerving situation facing the French government as it gathered under President de Gaulle on the afternoon of Monday, May 27: The referendum proposal had aroused nothing but derision and hostility; the Grenelle protocol had been thrown out by the workers; the strike had turned political with what appeared to be the support of the CGT. Paris—indeed the whole country—lived under the shadow of violence, uncertainty, and fear. It must have been one of the most painful Cabinet meetings of De Gaulle's ruthlessly well-ordered regime. With magnificent irrelevance the ministers examined and approved the text of the proposed referendum and the Grenelle protocol, both stillborn. Always resourceful, and believing that the day could still be saved if only the strike were broken, M. Pompidou called publicly on the union leaders to get their members to pronounce by secret ballot whether or not they wished to return to work. Later, when the strike was crumbling, these secret ballots were to prove a valuable

* Georges Séguy, in his report to the CGT National Confederal Committee, on June 13, 1968.

weapon in isolating the extremists. But with the crisis thundering to its summit, they were of little use.

The struggle in the capital was three-cornered. First, there was the government, with its troops, police, and civil servants—all the trappings of state power, but robbed of its substance by the crisis. Second, there was the official opposition, represented by the Communists (and the CGT, their union wing); the Socialists under François Mitterrand; and—a lonely but influential figure, whose star seemed in the ascendant—Pierre Mendès-France. Finally, there was the mixed bag of revolutionaries, and it is these we must now examine because Monday was their day.

In defiance of a government ban on demonstrations, Jacques Sauvageot, the UNEF leader, called a mass meeting that night at the Charléty Stadium in southern Paris. Contrary to expectation, a vast crowd assembled, at least 35,000 strong. This display of popular support for the young extremists was of considerable political importance. It marked the reentry of the student revolutionaries onto the national political stage after a period of eclipse in which initiative had seemed to pass into adult hands. The incredible success of the student leaders was to rally to the stadium thousands of young workers, disgruntled with the cautious, stick-in-the-mud union leadership. *"Séguy démission!"* they cried. The marriage of workers and students, longed for by all student revolutionaries, seemed to have come about. This was the apotheosis of the new left. In political terms it was the high point of the student movement, the moment when all the various revolutionary strands seemed most closely allied. And yet there was a touching innocence and indecisiveness about the leaders. They had been carried to this point by the élan of the movement, but they did not know what to do with the force they had created. "We are seeking a strategy, a political line; everyone is invited to speak freely and give his opinion," Jacques Sauvageot told the assembly.

The Charléty meeting gave the revolutionaries new heart, but their hope was founded on an illusion, and their analysis of the situation was confused. They clamored for De Gaulle's overthrow, and yet their chief target was not he, but the French Communist Party in which they had been raised and against which they now rebelled. They thought they were acting on the national plane and yet were irretrievably sectarian, caught in the petty doctrinal squabbles of French left-wing politics. Their cruelest shafts were directed against the CGT which they guyed as a "new ally" of the Gaullist state. Their loudest applause at Charléty was for André Barjonet, who had resigned from the CGT, where he was a top economic adviser, accusing its leaders of refusing to admit that France was in a revolutionary state. "Revolution today *is* possible!" he thundered, to the wild cheers of the youngsters. He was their biggest catch. Also on the platform was Jean-Pierre Vigier, expelled that weekend from the Communist Party for "anti-Party attitudes." A distinguished physicist, Vigier is a political hothead, displaying more courage than judgment. He became an active left-wing publicist, serving as secretary-general for the Russell Tribunal and as an officer of the *Comité Vietnam National*. Another "revolutionary personality" present was Alain Geismar, who had that day resigned from the teachers' union, SNESup, to devote himself full time to politics. Like Vigier, he is a physicist who has succumbed to the lure of extremist politics. In the crowd floated banners of the CFDT, the former Catholic union, which, unlike the CGT, was flirting with the revolutionaries. It saw in their dreams of *double pouvoir* a near cousin of its own claims for greater workers' control over management.

Only one orthodox political party lent its support to this anti- and extra-parliamentary rally: the *Parti Socialiste Unifié* (PSU), a small left-Socialist splinter group, squeezed uncomfortably between the federation and the Communist Party and loved by neither. Led by Michel Rocard and

Marc Heurgon, the PSU is a merger, dating back to 1961, of left-wing Catholics and other Marxists, who had fled from the Communist Party or from the SFIO. Theirs is a position of systematic contrariness. Both Jacques Sauvageot and Alain Geismar had been members; this encouraged the PSU to think that it could perhaps take over the vigorous student protest movement and harness it to its cause—an opportunistic attitude bitterly deplored by some of the young revolutionaries, for whom all established parties, including the PSU, are contemptible.

Although brand-new—indeed barely three weeks old— the revolutionary movement was already something of an anachronism; the political struggle was that week being played out between De Gaulle and the adult left. The young people who had detonated the crisis were deluded in thinking their role was still central. Moreover, although they all were revolutionaries, they were far from united. The Trotskyist JCR (whose *service d'ordre* led the vast crowd into the stadium—a delirious moment for a *groupuscule*) had little sympathy for Geismar or the PSU. The anarchists, who galloped into the stadium bearing their girl friends on their shoulders and black flags held high, had sympathy for no one. Indeed, the Charléty meeting would have been little more than an impressive example of lunatic-fringe politics were it not for the presence on the platform that night of one man: Pierre Mendès-France.

He was the left's "man of Providence," the conscience of French Social Democracy. Nominally a member of the PSU, he wished to identify himself with no party, but to hold himself ready for a call from the nation. Alone among leaders of the established left, he was quick to recognize the importance of the student revolt and sought to guide it into constructive channels out of its ghetto of bitterness and nihilism. It was this sympathy he was expressing by his presence at Charléty, but with characteristic ambivalence, he refused to speak. No doubt he thought there was some political capital to be picked up, but he could not have wished to be too closely associated with the blood and thunder spouted from the platform.

Nevertheless, his appearance at the revolutionary meeting was read by French opinion as the beginning of a political campaign. An independent contributor to *Le Monde,* Alfred Fabre-Luce, ended a column of fulsome praise for the statesman with the cry *"Mendès à l'Élysée."** Mendès-France was thought to be recruiting an army and posing his candidature for power. It was a spectacular reentry on the scene which could not be ignored by the other constituents of the adult left, namely M. Mitterrand and the Communists. To M. Mitterrand in particular, Mendès-France's reappearance after his long political hibernation was to prove of crucial importance, perhaps a curse, rather than a blessing.

As we saw in Chapter Thirteen, the crisis caught Mitterrand's federation unprepared: Its internal cohesion was uncertain, and its relationship with the Communists that of the weaker partner. M. Mitterrand had committed his federation to a betrothal with the CPF, but on the tacit understanding that the marriage would not be consummated until the federation was at least strong enough to hold its own. This was far from being the case, but the time had come for action. Mitterrand looked about him for an escape from the suffocating Communist embrace and saw Mendès-France. The two men had for ten years been resolutely opposed to the Gaullist regime. They both now called, in almost identical terms, for it to go. But they were not at one on all things. Mendès-France, the elder statesman, could not easily play second fiddle to Mitterrand who had served under him as Minister of the Interior in 1954-55. There was, therefore, a certain awkwardness in their relationship to do with Mitterrand's presidential ambitions, though this was not a major obstacle to their cooperation.

* *Le Monde* (May 29, 1968).

A more difficult problem was that the closer Mitterrand drew to Mendès, the less happy were the Communists. The CPF distrusted Mendès for his anti-Communist past; he was a member of the PSU, which they abhorred; he had befriended the young revolutionaries, who were anathema to them; he had let himself be seen at Charléty; finally, he posed as a "man of Providence" come to replace that other "man of Providence," De Gaulle. For the Communists, Mendès replacing De Gaulle was like De Gaulle replacing Pétain, a conception of rule totally different from the "popular government of democratic union" for which they strove.

Seeing Mitterrand slipping from their grasp, the Communists begged him on Monday to come to an immediate meeting to draft the basis of a common government program. But in spite of the urgency of Waldeck Rochet's plea, Mitterrand was evasive; he would not meet Rochet and his Politburo sooner than the afternoon of the following day, Tuesday, May 28, after he had addressed the press on Tuesday morning.

This was the tangled background to François Mitterrand's bid for power. Five hundred journalists crowded the Hôtel Continental to hear him pronounce the regime dead and himself a candidate for the Presidency. It was a clever package: scornful invective for faltering Gaullism (De Gaulle was dismissed as "the man of whom I shall say nothing today except that he can no longer make history"); a detailed plan for the succession; and a nice measure of idealism—France, in a new alliance of Socialism and liberty, was to provide the answer to the question posed earlier that spring in Prague.

The major premise of Mitterrand's argument was that the nation would say no to De Gaulle's referendum on June 16. He even envisaged the possibility of De Gaulle's quitting earlier. This would "naturally" be followed by the disappearance of the Prime Minister and his government. To fill the vacuum, Mitterrand proposed the immediate formation of a provisional government to put the state back on its feet and organize presidential elections. It would be a ten-man government, chosen *sans exclusion et sans dosage périmé*. This obscure but vital phrase meant roughly that the provisional administration would be formed without undue exclusiveness or outdated political bias. To head it, he proposed himself or Pierre Mendès-France, and as President of the republic he again proposed himself.

There was not much in this to give comfort to the Communists, and a good deal to disturb them. By his press conference Mitterrand, who had played virtually no role in the crisis because he could throw no troops into battle, now stepped to the center of the stage. It was a brilliant exercise in political illusionism. For a moment his Shadow Cabinet, listening to him from the front row, was all smiles as power seemed within its grasp. But Mitterrand made two mistakes, which were soon to count against him. His suggestion of a "provisional" government had a whiff of illegality about it. He did not adequately spell out the constitutional steps which Gaston Monnerville, President of the Senate and under the constitution Acting President of the republic in the event of De Gaulle's resignation, would have to take to appoint a new Prime Minister. In brief, Mitterrand laid himself open to the charge of planning a *coup d'état*. His second blunder was to seem to cast doubt on his alliance with the Communists, the one credible alternative to Gaullist rule. He named Mendès-France as future Premier but failed to refer to his Communist partners, except in the most elliptical terms. The curious phrase *sans dosage périmé* was no doubt a suggestion that the Communists, long excluded from power, should now be given a share; he called, too, on the new forces which had arisen not to overlook "the two powerful popular organizations which have led the struggle in difficult times"—clearly a reference to the Communists and to his own federation. But that was all.

Mitterrand had preferred the beguiling phantom of Mendès-France to the all too solid substance of the Communists, to whom he appeared to be changing horses in midstream. Their ancient fear that at the moment of decision he would rat on them, throwing over their long engagement and allying himself with someone else, seemed to be coming true.

Waldeck Rochet issued an angry statement on Tuesday afternoon. "There can be," he bluntly declared, "no left-wing policy of social progress without the active collaboration of the Communists. . . . We will not allow the replacement of the present regime by another . . . marking a return to a detestable past when governments claiming to be on the left pursued a policy of the right, excluding the working class and the Communist Party from the direction of the country affairs." The Communist Party, Rochet added, was ready to assume its government responsibilities and it "knows that this is what the workers want."

Thus, the Communists, in clear, even threatening terms, indicated their distaste for the Mitterrand-Mendès alliance and staked their own claim for a substantial share of power. Mitterrand's evasiveness had stung them into this bold, impatient demand. Meek and cautious in the past, courting respectability for so long, they now showed their hand. It was a major turning point in the crisis, and many of the subsequent developments flowed from it.

President de Gaulle and his government, analyzing the situation that Tuesday night, were driven to two inescapable conclusions: first, that all the forces of the official opposition—Mitterrand, Mendès-France, and the Communists—were now set to topple the regime; second, that in this constellation of forces, the Communists were overwhelmingly the strongest. They would dominate any government of which they were a part. Rumor has it that De Gaulle and his Prime Minister, Georges Pompidou, quarreled violently that night. The regime had touched bottom.

Whichever way it turned, the horizon seemed blocked. No one in Paris had yet shouted *"Vive De Gaulle!"* The suggestion is that Georges Pompidou told the President that, in order to save Gaullism, he, De Gaulle, would have to withdraw. Pompidou intended to fight on and considered the general at this stage an encumbrance.

No day in recent French history can match the anguish and excitement of Wednesday, May 29. The most skeptical minds came to believe that the regime was lost. The long, suspenseful day opened with the news that the weekly Cabinet meeting, held each Wednesday morning at ten as regularly as clockwork, was canceled. Ministers were turned away on the doorstep of the Élysée. The general saw no member of his government that morning, not even Pompidou. A little after eleven o'clock President and Mme. de Gaulle left the palace by car. Their destination was given as Colombey-les-deux-Églises, where the President has his country house. It was put about that he had gone to ponder a great decision in solitude. The news of his departure was greeted with consternation in government circles. Many Gaullists were near to giving up the ghost— or at least their party label. De Gaulle is thought to keep locked up in his safe at the Élysée his political testament— a statement for his successor on the future of France. It was said that before leaving the Élysée that Wednesday, he handed the key of the safe to his top aide, the secretary-general at the Presidency, Bernard Tricot. Large quantities of luggage were seen leaving the building. Had the great man at last decided to step down?

Consternation turned to panic—not without a touch of wild-humor—when, with the hours ticking by, De Gaulle failed to arrive at Colombey. He was lost. He had simply faded into the landscape. *"On a perdu le Général de Gaulle!"* radio reporters admitted with something like a hysterical giggle. And then the facts began gradually to leak out. He had driven with his wife to the heliport at

Issy-les-Moulineaux; three helicopters had taken off—one
a police machine, the second carrying the presidential couple
with a single aide-de-camp, a third laden with bodyguards.
Nothing is known of De Gaulle's mood at the time. Only
one phrase of his has been recorded, addressed to Mme.
de Gaulle as they boarded the aircraft: "*Dépéchez-vous,
madame, je vous en prie.*"

The general's exact itinerary that day is still in doubt.
He has not spoken, nor have his closest aides. What has
been established is that instead of heading for Colombey,
the three helicopters landed at a military airfield at St.-
Dizier, 125 miles east of Paris, halfway to the Rhine. The
presidential Caravelle had flown there to meet them from
strike-bound Orly. (According to an unconfirmed report,
he first called in at Taverny, the underground command
post of France's nuclear striking force, and spoke to various
military commanders over the secret communications network. According to yet another rumor, he was joined by his
son-in-law, General Alain de Boissieu, an army divisional
commander.) The Caravelle then headed east to land at
the military airport of Baden-Baden, headquarters of the
70,000 French troops in Germany. The West German
Chancellor, Kurt Kiesinger, was informed of the visit by
the French ambassador as the general touched down. No
representative of the federal government was there to
meet him, but protocol was not violated since, by tradition,
foreign heads of state can visit their troops stationed in
Germany without informing the German authorities.

De Gaulle did not leave the airfield but summoned
French army chiefs to meet him, including General Jacques
Massu, commander of French forces in Germany, and
General Beauvallet, military governor of Metz. What was
decided at this extraordinary council of war? No one knows
for certain, although speculation abounds. The most reli-
able sources suggest that the questions debated were of two
orders: the first, general and political; the second, military

and tactical. In Paris, De Gaulle had repeatedly consulted Pierre Messmer, Minister of the Armies, to ascertain from day to day the mood of the troops. Was the army loyal? Messmer, Army Minister for ten years and a pillar of the regime, is believed to have replied that the men could be relied on, but that it would be unwise to ask them to fire on civilians. In Baden-Baden, General Massu's professions of loyalty were forthright: The army was ready for any task the President assigned it. De Gaulle clearly considered his troops in Germany as a possible force of intervention, to be used if necessary to crush a Communist insurrection in the capital. A plan of campaign had to be drawn up, and the most loyal units—perhaps 20,000 men —moved to Metz ready for action. An operational headquarters was to be set up at Verdun.

In the weeks following the May crisis it was widely suggested that at the Baden-Baden meeting, De Gaulle's generals raised with him the continued detention since 1962 of General Raoul Salan, former head of the OAS—the murderous secret army which was dedicated to keep Algeria French. Did De Gaulle promise to wipe the OAS slate clean in return for General Massu's support? Was a gentleman's agreement reached? No one can be certain, but a fortnight later, on June 15, Salan and other OAS ringleaders were free men.

By 6:15 P.M. on Wednesday, May 29, General de Gaulle's helicopter put him down at Colombey with Mme. de Gaulle. But back in the capital, events sped on without him. In answer to the young revolutionaries' rally at Charléty on Monday, the orthodox left called its troops into the street that Wednesday afternoon under the enormous red and yellow banners of the CGT. Half a million workers paraded, sector by industrial sector, many in overalls, from the republican stronghold of the Bastille to the heart of Paris. Not a scuffle was reported. It was an impressive demonstration of disciplined workers' power. The marchers flooded the streets with the good humor of men who were winning. Carried on this human wave, the politicians of the left reached for the prize of the state. The spotlight turned on Mendès-France, the sad-eyed patriarch whose ten lonely years as Gaullism's most implacable critic had given him an unmatched moral stature. A Back Mendès committee was set up. Eugène Descamps, leader of France's second largest trade union federation, the CFDT, spoke out for him. Jean Lecanuet, a former presidential candidate and an influential politician of the center, called for a "government of public safety" and seemed to support Mendès-France's candidature.

At 6:35 P.M. on that day Mendès-France and Mitterrand came together to plan their capture of power. Guy Mollet, René Billères, and Gaston Defferre, top Socialist leaders turned midwives to help with the delivery of the new order, all were there. (Ten years earlier to the day, on May 29, 1958, Mollet had gone to Colombey to invite the general back to office.) Before night fell, Mendès-France had publicly declared in the lobbies of the National Assembly his willingness to accept whatever responsibilities a united left might confer upon him. Gaullism seemed no more, and its successor regime already half in place.

15   Triumph of Will

WHEN did General de Gaulle make his decision to fight back? He made it alone—probably during the night of Tuesday to Wednesday, May 28-29. What drove him at seventy-seven to this stupendous gathering of his resources? His government on Tuesday night was in total disarray, and his enemies were everywhere. Never had his fortunes sunk so low. He contemplated retirement, and his Prime Minister no doubt did little to dissuade him. Why then did he at dawn on Wednesday issue secret orders summoning the helicopters and the Caravelle which were to bear him to Germany? He went to Baden-Baden, we believe, already resolved to fight, not waiting for his generals to breathe courage into him. He went principally to concert plans for a military intervention in Paris, if it proved necessary. As a soldier-statesman, he never forgot that tanks can speak a language more persuasive than parliamentarians.

The extreme right in France, misled by the general's anti-Americanism and his flirtation with Russia, often accuses him of being overtolerant of Communism. The truth is quite the contrary; in pursuing his objective of grandeur and national independence for France, there is no fiercer opponent of the French Communist Party than General de Gaulle. All the evidence suggests that he was inspired to counterattack on Tuesday night when the Communists showed their hand. They said clearly they were determined to secure the share of power which was their due; they would no longer be excluded from government, and it was evident that neither Mitterrand nor Mendès-France could hold them. France was thus threatened with a Communist take-over. These were circumstances which left De Gaulle no choice. Retirement was unthinkable. He must stay on to save France, as he had done so often in the past. Such was no doubt his analysis. He must also have known that by speaking out, Waldeck Rochet had given him the weapon he needed to win: the great fear of Communism still widespread in France. On this interpretation, it was Mitterrand who, by flirting with Mendès and cold-shouldering the Communists, had stung the latter into speaking out, thus triggering De Gaulle's reflex, to which the whole of the left eventually fell victim. The trip to Baden-Baden, a necessary element in his counterattack, may also have satisfied the general's sense of drama; he may not have been unhappy at the thought of the whole world waiting in suspense on his movements.

On his return to Colombey on Wednesday night, De Gaulle in the solitude of his study drafted the short speech, which the next day was to put him back in business. He also made a few telephone calls, no one knows exactly to whom, except that overnight a profound change came over some key Gaullists, who so recently had been floundering in despair. A straw in the wind, hardly noticed by the still euphoric left on Thursday morning, was the statement— surprisingly confident in the circumstances—by Robert Poujade, secretary-general of the ruling Gaullist party. "The government," he declared, "will not yield to subversion, and the dreams of the usurpers will soon fade." Poujade, a young academic turned politician (no relation to the leader of the shopkeepers' movement in the early fifties), had at forty become a keyman of the regime. Pompidou's influence had made him the full-time boss of the party machine.

Pompidou too knew that De Gaulle was returning to Paris in fighting mood that Thursday morning, but he could not guess what tactical plans the general had up his sleeve. He had not been informed in advance of the Baden-Baden trip; he did not know whether De Gaulle had now been persuaded that his referendum was unworkable and that only the promise of elections would pacify opinion; above all, he could not be sure that his own job was safe.

Apart from the one or two Gaullist faithfuls, no one had the slightest notion what to expect. Even a man as close to the center of power as Valéry Giscard d'Estaing, leader of the Independent Republicans, with two ministers in the government, was that Thursday morning in the dark. In a public statement he declared himself in favor of De Gaulle's remaining at the head of the state but called for the departure of Pompidou and fresh elections. The story going the rounds in French political circles that morning was "the two Georges have failed"—Georges Séguy, the CGT leader who had been stampeded by his rank and file, and Georges Pompidou, whose Herculean efforts had failed to control a runaway situation.

By late morning De Gaulle was back in the capital. All France waited in terrible suspense for his verdict. The Assembly was in a fever. In the dining hall, deputies lunched with transistor sets held to their ears. At 2:30 the general received the Prime Minister alone. (Rumor has it that Pompidou, beside himself at being kept in the dark, said, "This is intolerable! I'm resigning!" To which the President good-humoredly retorted, *"Allons, mon vieux!* Let's talk seriously. What about those elections you always wanted?") Half an hour later, their black, whalelike Citroëns nosing into the courtyard of the Élysée, De Gaulle's twenty-seven ministers arrived for what for some was to be their last Cabinet meeting. Even as they gathered, corteges of hooting cars, bristling with Tricolors, roared their way down the Faubourg St.-Honoré in front of the Élysée Palace, strewing the pavements with tracts calling on the population to demonstrate for De Gaulle in the Place da la Concorde that afternoon. Robert Poujade had done his job well.

Then, at 4:31 P.M., De Gaulle spoke to the nation. In four and a half terse, brutal minutes, he smashed the left's dreams of immediate power. He was going to fight. He barked out his sentences as if on a parade ground. He had in the past twenty-four hours considered all possibilities and had now made up his mind. "In the present circumstances I will not withdraw. I have a mandate from the people. I will fulfill it." He would not change his Prime Minister, but the Cabinet would be reshuffled. The National Assembly would be immediately dissolved, and general elections held. The proposed referendum would be deferred. The country, he said, was threatened with Communist dictatorship. This "totalitarian enterprise" wished France to resign herself to a power imposed in the midst of national despair. *"Eh bien! Non!"* The republic would not abdicate. Civic action in defense of the republic must be set on foot "everywhere and at once" to help the government in Paris and the prefects in the provinces—renamed on the spot commissioners of the republic, a reference to the title they assumed with wide powers at the Liberation. If the trial of strength continued, he was ready to use "other means." Here was the hint of troops, the threat of force, the shadow of General Massu.

De Gaulle's secret weapon, his power over words, had this time not failed him to the immense relief of his supporters. They felt they had been snatched from the abyss. But there was not a word in the speech about the legitimate claims of the striking workers or about the aspirations of youth; nothing but a fierce and compelling contempt for his compatriots and a stark anti-Communism unknown since the early days of the cold war. But what an astounding comeback! "After twenty-four hours of mystery and incredible suspense, the tragic hero springs, with words defiant, from the trapdoor through which the pretender to the succession had thought him gone forever."*

Barely had his fierce *Vive la France!* died away when Gaullist supporters flooded the streets on their way to the Concorde. The general had struck the note to which the "party of fear"—the massed hordes of conservative France —responded. In its search for support, the regime pulled out all the stops. In its hour of need, it did not heed whether the men it called out into the street were old Pétainists, or supporters of General Salan, or Maurrasian nationalists, heirs of Vichy and French Algeria. The common fear of Communism brought together the extreme right and left-wing Gaullism and every shade of opinion in between. In that moment of panic, the regime changed its nature or at least its image. Busloads of supporters were brought in posthaste from the provinces to swell the demonstration, the coaches waiting in the side streets until the picnic was over.

The human flood poured through the funnel of the Place de la Concorde into the Champs-Élysées, heading for the Eternal Flame at the Étoile, the symbol of undying nationalism. It doubled the Communists' turnout of the day before, trumping the formidable CGT card. Most collars in the crowd were clean; medals were worn; many of the women wore gloves and were of an age to remember De Gaulle's triumphant progress down that splendid avenue at the Liberation. *"Le communisme ne passera pas!"* they chanted, but also offensive slogans like *Cohn-Bendit à Dachau!* and *La France aux français!* At last the right, so long silent, had descended into the street, borrowing the style and methods of the left. Instead of clenched fists, they raised their hands in the V for victory sign. Instead of the "Internationale," they tirelessly sang the "Marseillaise."

* Sirius (Hubert Beuve-Mery, the editor), in *Le Monde* (June 1, 1968).

The Tricolor triumphed over the red and black flags. The whole emotional scene was colored red, white, and blue.

That afternoon the general wrote in his own hand to Jacques Chaban-Delmas and Gaston Monnerville, the presidents of the Chamber of Deputies and of the Senate, informing them that their assemblies were dissolved. Wild scenes followed, with the opposition standing to sing the "Marseillaise." François Mitterrand was the first to react to De Gaulle's speech: "This is dictatorship," he declared. "It is a call to civil war." But Gaullist ministers and deputies donned their parliamentary scarves and marched under the Tricolor to join the demonstration at the Concorde. The regime, lapped in a warm tide of loyalty, felt safe.

The will of the general flowed like fuel to the whole government machine. The state fought back for the authority which had in the past three weeks fallen from it. Christian Fouchet, Minister of the Interior, telephoned personally to each of the regional *préfets,* urging them to stand firm. It was one of his last tasks as minister before being axed in Pompidou's government reshuffle the following day. As the counterrevolution set in, the mood of the country changed with lightning speed. In the Gaullist demonstration, Mitterrand had been abused as a public enemy. That night a band of Gaullist rowdies chased him into a doorway at St.-Germain-des-Prés, but he was rescued and escorted home by sympathetic students.

Troop movements were reported around Paris, and tanks were seen on country roads. It was announced that skilled reservists would be called up to run essential services. Paramilitary committees of civic action sprang up here and there across the country, on one or two occasions celebrating their legitimized thuggery by firing a few shots at trade union or Communist Party office buildings. Before dawn on Friday, May 31, armed police occupied the central post office at Rouen, throwing out the workers' pickets. This was the first attempt to break the strikes, beginning with the weak sectors like postal workers.

Government-sponsored secret ballots set rolling a patchy back-to-work movement. From plant after plant came news of strikers sitting down to talk to employers. After a brief spell of freedom, the state radio's tone seemed subtly to change as commentators trimmed to the new situation. But it was the Communist Party and its great trade union federation, the CGT, which faced the most agonizing adjustment. In a giant game of poker, De Gaulle had raised the stakes. To challenge his legitimacy now was to tumble into the insurrection which they had been at such pains to avoid. Wednesday's political slogans, the cries for a government of the people, were quietly buried. By Friday all the French unions had said they were ready to talk to the government about their economic claims without preconditions. Overnight the strike was stripped of politics.

The left, both Socialist and Communist, was thrown off-balance by the vigor of De Gaulle's assault. It was paralyzed by his unfair charge that it had plotted revolution. This was precisely what the Communists had sought to avoid. As for Mitterrand, he had perhaps been hasty, but never subversive. To save himself, De Gaulle tarred both Socialists and Communists with conspiracy, casting them beyond the pale of the republic, and calling on ordinary citizens to arm and strike them down. Thus he united his own supporters but divided the country as never before. Backing down from a crude trial of strength with the general, the left threw itself into campaigning for the elections which it had forced him to concede. But it was grossly handicapped from the start by having to refute his charges before a public traumatized and confused by the violence of the preceding month. A new phase of the struggle opened, but those of the left were losers all the way. "We have not changed," the Communist Party said to its militants as it swung around 180 degrees. "Life has."

16   Counterrevolution at the Polls

FAR from overthrowing General de Gaulle, the May Revolution gave his regime a new and powerful lease of life. On May 29 he seemed finished; a little more than a month later, following the elections of June 23 and June 30, he was back in the saddle with a parliamentary majority unrivaled in the history of republican France. In the months since the crisis, men have been totting up its cost, gloomily weighing the damage to French industry, to the franc, to France's external position, to the President's image. But it could equally well be argued that the explosion was a salutary shake-up which sent the blood coursing again through the hardening arteries of French society. More thoroughly than any government investigation, the revolt identified the ills from which France was suffering and, in the subsequent electoral triumph, gave the general the means to put them right. Few statesmen have been so fortunate.

It is scarcely remembered now that barely a month before the crisis the country was in a sort of stagnant, unfertile calm which prompted a leading commentator, Pierre Viansson-Ponté of *Le Monde,* to write that France was bored. Internally, the regime had lost its impetus and its sense of direction; after ten years of rule it was complacent, rather than creative. The general was showing undeniable signs of age, daily delegating more authority to his dauphin, Pompidou, and the principal subject of conversation in political Paris was *l'après-gaullisme*. After the June, 1968, elections no one could any longer complain of boredom. A rejuvenated De Gaulle was preparing to embark on a brand-new phase of his astounding career, involving the profound restructuring of French social and industrial relationships. This, then, was one of the paradoxes of the May Revolution: Far from ending De Gaulle's rule, it prolonged it and gave it a new purposefulness.

The moment was rich in paradox: A classic parliamentary election came to put an end to a crisis which was, in essence, extra-parliamentary, unfolding in the street in defiance or neglect of traditional political forms; the Communist Party was accused of conspiracy when it had worn itself out in seeking to quell troublemaking conspirators on its left; the general was carried back to power by a massive right-wing vote on what was—in so far as it was spelled out—a left-wing program of reforms; Georges Pompidou, the principal architect of victory, was almost immediately afterward dismissed from office by the general. But we are anticipating.

The Gaullist triumph was the fruit of two broad trends: one springing immediately from the May crisis; the other no more than the continuing pattern of French politics. Even without the crisis, had elections been held in June, 1968, the Gaullists would no doubt have won them—but less massively. The skill of the government strategists was to turn the revolution exclusively to their own account. No matter that the outburst showed up the failures of a decade of Gaullist rule and the incapacity of the government in a moment of crisis. By harping solely on the bogeys of violence and Communist plots, the government turned the revolution from a liability into a colossal electoral asset. This strategy brought in the votes, but at the cost of the truth. It misrepresented the revolution, picturing it in the most lurid colors as a Communist-inspired contest for power, which it never was, not even by accident, and ignoring the thirst for liberty and professional autonomy which had powered the explosion.

In spite of the striking millions, the revolution was the work of an intellectual elite: students and professional men —all those who understood that France, in a thousand sectors of life, needed freeing from the dead hand of bureaucracy and petty regulation. This was the profound sense of the revolt, but only an active minority grasped it. The workers joined the movement in support of their own, very different, largely material, claims. Some young workers at the base of the union machines were touched by a revolutionary spirit, and, as we have seen, the CFDT for instance campaigned for structural reforms in industry of an extremely radical nature. But these ideas made little impact on a working class committed in its overwhelming majority to the pursuit of greater material comforts and benefits within the structure of society as at present organized. The mass of the French population did not begin to understand the feeling of cultural suffocation which had driven intellectuals to rebel. At first confused and bewildered by the disturbances in the capital, most people soon became profoundly alarmed. They were gripped by a great fear which General de Gaulle's black-and-white analysis on May 30 only confirmed. When he spoke of Communist subversion, the violence they watched with horror and incomprehension on their television screens was suddenly made clear. Few people in the country distinguished between the Communist Party and the revolutionary *groupuscules*, linking them together as a common menace, although they were bitter enemies. Every barricade cost the opposition thousands of votes.

The election campaign was short and singularly uninformative. None of the candidates put forward a detailed program but concentrated, instead, on slandering and discrediting his opponents. M. Pompidou set the pace for the campaign and chose the ground on which to fight. "Supposing," he declared, in a broadcast on the eve of the poll, "that the united left had won [last year]. M. Mitterrand would be in the Élysée; the Communists would have entered the government; and the Communist Party, as it has done everywhere and everywhere successfully, would slowly but implacably have extended its hold to the point of dictatorship. Then either M. Mitterrand would have given in, which I think most probable, or he would have tried to oppose them, and as we saw happen some years ago in Prague, would have been pushed out of the window. Today the red flag would be flying over the Élysée, over Matignon, over every town hall in France. . . ." To drive home this point, the Gaullists constituted themselves for the elections into the Union for the Defense of the Republic (UDR)—the new name suggesting that they alone were the custodians of republican freedoms, that they alone held high the Tricolor over the evil black and red flags of the opposition. With such bloodcurdling evocations the elections were won.

In the face of this assault, the left was thrown on the defensive. Pompidou's strategy was skillfully directed at its two weakest points: the Communist-Socialist alliance and the internal cohesion of Mitterrand's Socialist federation. By denouncing the Communists as untouchables, he put the alliance under great strain, sending some members of the federation heading toward the center in their panic to dissociate themselves from the Communist pariahs. This is where the May crisis did no more than highlight tensions which, as we saw in Chapter Thirteen, long antedated it. The ill fortune of the federation was to have been overtaken by the crisis when it was engaged in a slow process of transformation and unification. As we have said many times, it was not ready for it and now, in the election campaign, had to pay the price. Waldeck Rochet, confident in the support of a traditional Communist electorate, conducted a stolid, unspectacular campaign, in which he sought to reassure the electorate that the Communist Party had neither horns nor a tail. Mitterrand's task was more difficult; he was passionate, pleading, eloquent—but to no avail. He had to pretend his federation was united, when both Félix Gaillard, the Radical leader, and Gaston Defferre, the moderate Socialist mayor of Marseilles, among many others, made only too clear that they disputed the alliance with the Communists on which Mitterrand's long-term strategy was based, but which he had himself so tragically compromised during the crisis. These were not the only troubles of the left. The PSU on its flank brought comfort to the Gaullists by lashing out venomously against both Communists and Socialists, as did the student guerrillas in their myriad factions. The left had not been so divided for a decade. These, then, were the explanations for the Gaullist landslide: fear; the hatred of Communism; the fragmentation of the left. Where the left split under the strain of the crisis, the right in contrast closed its ranks. The freeing from jail and amnesty of the OAS leaders little more than a week before the elections reconciled, for the first time in a decade, the forces which put De Gaulle in power in 1958—a bitter outcome which the student revolutionaries could scarcely have anticipated.

Everything favored the Gaullists, even the static background to the elections. For twenty years the left had been losing favor with the electorate, while the right and center gained ground. On the morrow of the Liberation, 65 percent of Frenchmen voted for the left; in June, 1968, no more than 42.6. Gaullism, traditionally loosely structured, more of a personality cult than an organization, was for the first time in 1968 a disciplined, tightly knit political party. This, too, counted at the polls. In a political spectrum, increasingly bipolar, the Gaullist right was well drilled and centrally directed, responding as one man to the electoral strategy of Georges Pompidou and Robert Poujade, whereas their opponents were like a tribal army under a dozen petty chieftains. One further point deserves mention: The French electorate may be sheep, as De Gaulle is alleged to have said, but it is not entirely without sense. The crude fact last June was that the governing team of Pompidou, Couve de Murville, Michel Debré, Pierre Messmer, and all their colleagues, headed by the general himself, seemed far more competent and reassuring than the men fielded by the opposition, who either appeared like ghosts from the discredited Fourth Republic or else were young and untried. The voting public may well have thought that if radical reforms were necessary, De Gaulle, alerted and chastened by the crisis, was more likely to bring them about.

Nothing which happened in the twenty-three days between De Gaulle's dissolution of Parliament on May 30 and the first round of the elections on June 23 brought comfort to the opposition. The revolt was not immediately extinguished with De Gaulle's fighting speech, nor did the workers immediately take up their tools. Here and there a spontaneous return to work occurred, but most of the factories of France stayed closed and occupied well into June, and Renault, the bastion of the strike, did not yield until June 18, nearly five weeks after the first wildcat rebellion at Nantes on May 14. Right across French industry the Grenelle agreements were used as a "platform" from which to negotiate still greater wage benefits—increases of between 10 and 14 percent at Renault, already the highest paying industry in the country; but the CFDT's tentative claim for workers' power in the plants was nowhere conceded. The Great Strike of May, 1968, gave everyone a fatter wage package and in many cases a shorter working week, but it resulted in no profound changes in management-worker relationships.

The crumbling of the strike was accompanied by savage outbreaks of violence. On Monday, June 10, the opening day of the election campaign, a seventeen-year-old schoolboy, Gilles Tautin, a member of the pro-Chinese UJC-

(M-L), was drowned in the Seine near Flins, fleeing before a police charge. He had come to encourage the Renault strikers besieged by riot police called up by the management. His drowning triggered a night of brutal skirmishing in Paris. There were the usual barricades of cobblestones and sawn-down plane trees, the usual toll of injuries and wholesale arrests. What was new was that the demonstrators took to the roofs, showering the police with slates and Molotov cocktails. Five police stations were attacked to the cry of *"Ils ont tué nos camarades!"* At dawn on Tuesday morning a young worker was killed, shot through the chest, at Peugeot's Sochaux plant in eastern France. Here, too, the management had called in the riot police. No one knows who fired the bullet, but only the police had guns. A second Sochaux workman cracked his skull (and died a day later) in a scramble to escape a police charge. In Paris a protest demonstration, called on Tuesday night by the students' union, led the police in a savage game of hide-and-seek across the city. Never in a month of almost nightly disorder did the fighting range so widely on both banks of the Seine or last so long. The fire brigade was that night called out 300 times. Seventy-five private cars and ten police vans were wrecked. Twenty-five ancient and splendid trees were cut down. Seventy-two barricades were thrown up in streets miles apart, as demonstrators stood, fought, then fled light-footedly before their more heavily armed adversaries. Tens of thousands of Parisians spent a sleepless night, shattered by explosions as in an artillery bombardment. These were the death throes of the student revolt, their last wild gestures of defiance at the Gaullist regime, but they were also nails in the coffin of the left's electoral hopes.

On Wednesday, June 12, confident of public approval, the government banned all demonstrations throughout France until the elections and dissolved and declared illegal a dozen extremist organizations, the most important of which were the Trotskyist JCR, FER, *Voix Ouvrière*, PCI, and OCI, the pro-Chinese UJC(M-L) and PCMLF, and Cohn-Bendit's March 22 Movement.* The JCR, perhaps the most powerful of the groups and the best prepared for clandestinity, drew its funds from the bank ahead of the police; the FER and the UJC(M-L) were less fortunate. Alain Krivine, the JCR leader, went underground but was arrested a month later in Paris on July 16. "Our policy," M. Pompidou declared, "is patience and firmness—with a little more firmness every day." Gradually the government recovered state property held by the revolutionaries, and the red flag was hauled down. Scores of troublesome foreigners were summarily expelled, drawing, in the case of West German citizens, protests from the Bonn government.

Another disturbing feature of the government's election campaign was the encouragement of Committees of Civic Action in the provinces—in many cases armed rowdies, who disturbed the peace with gunfire in Orléans, Rouen, and La Rochelle. In Guy Mollet's constituency of Arras an eighteen-year-old Communist canvasser was shot dead on June 29, the eve of the final round of the elections, by government supporters.

Some 28,400,000 voters had to choose between 2,267 candidates for 487 seats. The Gaullists won the first round on June 23 and triumphed at the second on June 30, while the left was defeated and then routed. Alone and without need of allies, the UDR won 295 seats (against 197 in the previous Parliament), a bumper 51 seats more than required to secure an absolute majority. Giscard d'Estaing's Independent Republicans—Gaullists, but not "unconditional"—won a further 64 seats (against 43), making them the second largest group in the Assembly. Whereas, in the previous Assembly, Georges Pompidou needed Giscard d'Estaing's reluctant support to make up his majority, now he could rule without him. The Federation of the Left

* For details of these organizations, see Chapter Two.

kept a meager 57 seats (against 118), and the Communists only 34 (against 73). The PSU was wiped out, losing its 3 deputies. As for Jacques Duhamel's *Progrès et Démocratie Moderne* (PDM) in the center, it finally scraped together 30 seats (against 42), the minimum necessary to form a parliamentary group. François Mitterrand described the results as "an operation in political and psychological trickery," and Waldeck Rochet described them as "an important step on the road to Fascism." His number two, Georges Marchais, added, "It's all Cohn-Bendit's fault."

North of the Loire and south of it, in every corner of France, the Gaullists gained seats, often in opposition strongholds where they had never penetrated before. In the capital they captured all seats except one. Pierre Mendès-France, who a month earlier had seemed so close to power, was beaten at Grenoble by a narrow majority of 132 votes. M. Mitterrand's friends were the great losers (in terms of seats, if not of votes). All sixteen of his young "lieutenants" —members of the Convention of Republican Institutions —who had entered Parliament in 1967 were this time eliminated. Socialists and Communists together lost 100 seats—the gravest setback suffered by the parliamentary left in its history. François Mitterrand contemplated the utter collapse of his hopes of presenting the electorate with a credible alternative on the left to General de Gaulle. With his own position under attack, he now has to rebuild the federation virtually from scratch, forging it into a unified party, not just a loose association of mildly antagonistic "political families." He must consider how valid for the future is his strategy of an electoral alliance with the Communists which so many voters clearly disavowed. Never have the Communists seemed farther from achieving power in France through parliamentary means. As a parliamentary party, they are back in the ghetto from which they had striven so hard to emerge over the last five years.

One of the surprises of the May crisis was the extent to which young people were won over to the view that direct action in the streets was more effective than action in Parliament. This dangerous trend could gain further ground if a Gaullist-dominated Parliament proves to be even more of a rubber stamp than it was in the last session. Was it an accident that the Latin Quarter, the students' stronghold, had the highest percentage of abstentions (35.6 percent) at the June, 1968, elections? Was it not significant that a third of the electors was over fifty-five years old? The massed ranks of Gaullist deputies—a mini-Parliament on their own rather than a maxi-majority, as one commentator put it—camouflaged the revolution's legacy of bitterness and the profound cleavage in the country.

But to a remarkable extent the June elections and their results are irrelevant to the future course of French affairs. Under the Gaullist system the President shares his authority with no one. Neither his new 300-strong parliamentary majority nor the loyal barons of the regime have any political reality apart from himself. Rarely was this truth so clearly demonstrated as in the general's abrupt dismissal of his Prime Minister, Georges Pompidou, on July 10, 1968. His position as De Gaulle's accredited dauphin had seemed as certain as anything could be in politics. At the height of the crisis on May 30 De Gaulle declared, "I will not change my Prime Minister," adding a glowing personal tribute. The next day Pompidou reshuffled his Cabinet, dropping a number of ministers who had come under fire in the crisis (even if they had been doing no more than carrying out De Gaulle's instructions). Maurice Couve de Murville (Foreign Minister) and Michel Debré (Minister of Finance), two stalwarts of the regime, simply swapped posts. The new team seemed set for a long run. Six weeks later Pompidou himself fell from grace, ten days after the landslide victory at the polls for which he could so justly take the credit. It was a political beheading worthy of the Ottoman court.

After six years as Prime Minister, Pompidou was the one man in France apart from the general to wear the magic mantle known as political authority. His office at the Hôtel Matignon had become a very considerable source of influence and patronage. The affluence in its antechambers sometimes made the Élysée seem a little remote and neglected. Pompidou had placed his men in many key positions, and his ideas were beginning to influence high policy. But he was guilty of one great crime: popularity, a gift conferred from below, not bestowed from above. And so, with a stroke of the pen, De Gaulle broke him. Maurice Couve de Murville, a great servant of the state, if not a statesman, took his place. He would take no sun off the President.

Very crudely speaking, 1958 to 1962 marked the "Algerian phase" of President de Gaulle's Herculean enterprise of hoisting France into the front rank of nations. His instrument at the time was the fiery, inflexibly loyal, prodigiously hardworking Michel Debré. The second phase, 1962 to 1968, has been termed "institutional," to mark the consolidation and legitimization of the Fifth Republic in a series of elections, of which June's was the most decisive. This was Georges Pompidou's achievement. Now the third, or "social," phase may be opening under the direction of Couve de Murville, an outstanding technocrat. It appears that President De Gaulle has set his heart on steering France on an original course, halfway between capitalism and Communism, free from the evils of either, and of which the magic slogan is "Participation. "

The odds are that De Gaulle is planning, in his wily old age, another profitable raid on the ideas and philosophies of the left. Reinforced in power by an immense conservative vote, he may be about to attempt a radical transformation of French society which the routed leaders of French Socialism could well envy. It is an amazing demonstration of political virility in a man of seventy-seven.

Conclusions

DE GAULLE's triumphant restoration leaves two questions unanswered: Could the May Revolution happen again? And is the fever contagious? Only by understanding what really happened in France can we begin to resolve these puzzles. The phenomenon we have tried to describe was complex, and we cannot be sure to have identified even its most important elements beneath their extravagant camouflage of poetry, sex, and nonsense. Perhaps one of the first and simplest things to say is that the revolution was not a political crisis in the classic sense. It was not until its very final stages—and then almost by accident—a bid for political power.

What has confused many observers is that the revolution was made up of a great number of interwoven strands, each with its own specific nature, but not easily isolated from the others. For example, the JCR and Cohn-Bendit's March 22 Movement—the two principal detonators of the explosion —were avowedly revolutionary, representing the revival in French politics of the cult of direct, extra-parliamentary action. They and their fellow *groupuscules* drew their inspiration from philosophers of violence; Trotsky, in particular, dead for a quarter of a century, reemerged as a living influence. His followers believe that the industrial working class of Western Europe, long lulled by the prizes of a consumer society, is ready once more for a revolutionary role. Hence the Trotskyists' fury at the Communist Party and the Communist-led CGT, accused of stifling this vocation.

But the aims and state of mind of these revolutionaries were of a totally different nature from those of the thousands of French intellectuals who fervently joined the protest movement. Theirs was a painful awareness of the deprivations which organized society imposes on human beings. They rebelled against the humbug of French intellectual life, the pomp of officialdom, the social pressures of a bourgeois society. They wanted to throw everything over and think it all out anew. Their thirst for freedom from meaningless constraints broke out into high-minded manifestos and found practical expression in scores of action committees whose only common philosophy was that society as at present organized was intolerable and had to be remade. The unrest reached the professional classes, changing its nature once more because it was directed against the rigid, archaic, overcentralized structures in which most highly trained Frenchmen have to work. In this form, it was a revolt against ruling bureaucracies, administrative machines, professional apparatuses. It found expression in an urge to run one's own affairs—a need to dispose of oneself in the face of petty tyranny in office and laboratory, in hospital and university. This aspect of the disturbance was specifically French—because French professional life is more hidebound than most—but it was also this which suggested that what happened in May was the first full-scale challenge in a Western state to the inhuman efficiency of modern industrial life. It was compared to the utopian rebellions against the first Industrial Revolution.

The most familiar—because traditional—face of the revolution was the strike. But in spite of the spectacular occupations of factories and the locking up of managers, in spite of the CFDT's suggestion that boards of directors should be elected and dismissed by a poll like a town council, in spite of the restive young workers eager to escape from the cautious hand of union control, it was just a good old-fashioned strike for bigger take-home earnings and a shorter working week. Locked up with their machines and dreaming of their summer holidays, the strikers had nothing remotely in common with the revolutionary theorists of the JCR, except as links in a turbulent chain of events.

Hounded by the young revolutionaries, the undisciplined students, the rebellious professional men, and the sullen strikers, the regime faltered. It was then that the official left-wing opposition stepped on to the stage to go through the ritual acts expected of an opposition. Leaning on a door which began to open, it could not help falling through it. This was the phase at which the crisis turned "political," nearly overthrowing De Gaulle. But this spectacular turn was little more than an accidental byproduct of the May Revolution and certainly not the result of a conspiracy. If proof were required, it need only be observed that the Socialists were painfully unprepared for the crisis and that the Communists turned their back on power when given a tempting chance to grab at it. Moreover, had DeGaulle fallen and been replaced in due course by M. Mitterrand, under the procedures provided by the constitution, this would have been just another transfer of power in the age-old political game: no revolution—or at least not one which a genuine rebel would recognize.

De Gaulle survived because no one, until the very last moment, ever really thought he would fall. Nobody set out determinedly to topple him, because no one believed it could be done. In this the Communists were more lucid than most. It is not easy to overthrow masters of highly organized, thoroughly centralized states. They hold in their hands too great a concentration of economic and military power. Defied by the strikers, De Gaulle flew to Germany, as if as a reminder that the ultimate military weapon was still his, and his enemies climbed down. The crisis thus threw fresh light on the element of brutality in De Gaulle's thinking and on the realistic political tradition to which he belongs. Never was his Caesarism—his sublime contempt for the masses, his heroic and yet tragic glorifying of authority—so displayed as in his May 30 speech. Never was the hollowness of French parliamentary democracy so vividly demonstrated as by the sacking of Pompidou on the morrow of the electoral triumph. The elections were thus revealed in their true nature, as a referendum confirming the untrammeled powers of the head of state.

The crisis threw an equally bright light on the opposition. The Communist Party did not attempt to seize power, because it was no longer in its nature to be revolutionary. It mouthed slogans about class struggle but no longer believed them. Over the passage of years it has become a sober workers' party, mesmerized with cars and television sets, the French equivalent of the British Labour Party. May, 1968, revealed to public gaze that the de-Stalinization of the CPF, obscured by the continuity of the leadership and the Central Committee's tradition of secrecy, had in fact taken place. The party was, however, still strong: It controlled newspapers, municipalities, trading companies, and a score of cultural, sports, and youth organizations. Thousands of men depended directly on it for their livelihood. But it was no longer a fighting party. In seeking to adjust to a modern, increasingly classless and affluent society, its revolutionary past was more a liability than an asset.

As for its alleged stranglehold over the French economy exercise through its union arm, the CGT, the crisis also exposed the fallacy of this charge. The truth is that, when the test came, the union organization proved too weak, rather than too strong. On Monday, May 27, the Grenelle agreements, although accepted by the CGT leaders, were thrown out by the rank and file, which thus dragged the

Communist Party into a brief political adventure which it had done everything in its power to avoid and which, as it feared, resulted in its slaughter at the polls.

What of the revolutionaries? Throughout the crisis the various sects attempted to come together within the framework of a newly formed revolutionary movement, on the argument that all the inflammable tinder which the events of May had demonstrated was lying about should be gathered up for future use. But the proposed movement collapsed under the weight of personal and doctrinal rivalries. It was one of many false starts. It is possible that the size of the bang set off by their spark misled the revolutionaries into thinking their big moment had come. But the suffocating intellectuals, disgruntled professional men, overcrowded students, and striking workers had, for the most part, other, wholly reformist ambitions. This is why when the revolutionaries accuse the Communist Party of betraying the "revolution," it is like deaf men talking to each other. Modern states are not so vulnerable to the Cohn-Bendits of this world as the dramatic nature of the barricades might make one suppose. Indeed, every fire lit in the streets is a vote cast for the right at the next election.

The Gaullist state may be strong, but, no more than any other society, does it really know where it is going or how its human community will tomorrow be organized? For a decade, perhaps even much longer, the French have not asked themselves fundamental questions about the nature of their society. They have allowed it to be shaped, often inhumanely, by the scramble to modernize, industrialize, become competitive. A few banal words by De Gaulle during the crisis on the need to seek a middle course between capitalism and Communism were immediately seized on as stimulating and profound—surely a key to the poverty of earlier thinking on the subject.

But there was a more hopeful side to the May Revolution. It released a torrent of critical energy that for a moment made officialdom cringe and left every emperor naked. It carried the germ of hope that the intellect, the spirit, and the imagination, if given free range and scope, could really change the world.

INDEX